Praise

Letters Acr
A journey of enlightenment

"This latest work by Stephen Chong, *Letters Across Time: A journey of enlightenment* is very special and beautifully written! Love and wisdom beam off the pages. Through the medium of story-telling and the delightful duck-pond tales Chong encourages us to reach across time to delve deeper into ourselves and our own Book of Mysteries. This work is both timely as it is providential. Enjoy it! It's fresh and exciting!"
Ancilla Fasciolla BOccThy - Queensland Health

"Chong, in *Letters Across Time* shows yet again, that he is an inspirational writer who knows how to move and enable the reader and how to leave the world a better place."
Letizia C De Rosa - Director of Book Creators Circle

"Stephen Chong's new book, *Letters Across Time*, is a testament to his writing style and to his sense of the spiritual. As he says, it is designed to help the reader discover, within themself, the motivation and inspiration to realise his or her highest potential in life. It contains the continuing story of Benjamin Duck and his descendants, taken from his previous book *The Music of the Soul* (2011). But it is interspersed with telling short stories and quotations designed to inspire. Good reading for the new age reader or just for those who are interested in the higher dimensions to life."
Graham Nicholson, Hidden Words Bookshop

"What I love most about Chong's books is that no matter where you're at in your life, there are always opportunities to take away

a message that you need right now. Then the next time you feel stuck or dissatisfied in any way, you can re-read his books and find a different lesson that will help you initiate change."
Wendy Ackland

Stories – fairytales, folktales, parables, myths, allegories – since time immemorial, have been the means of imparting wisdom and used as a mode of transformation. Such tales can entertain us, make us think, trip the mind or access and stimulate the place within us from which all wisdom arises.

In *Letters Across Time*, Stephen has again with an inspired allegory, interspersed with cogent parables, brought to all who read it, the way to that place that resides in all of us.
The Universal Storyteller

Letters Across Time:

A Journey of Enlightenment

Stephen Chong M.Ed.

Letters Across Time:

A Journey of Enlightenment

Stephen Chong M.Ed.

BOOKS

Winchester, UK
Washington, USA

First published by O-Books, 2013
O-Books is an imprint of John Hunt Publishing Ltd., Laurel House, Station Approach,
Alresford, Hants, SO24 9JH, UK
office1@jhpbooks.net
www.johnhuntpublishing.com

For distributor details and how to order please visit the 'Ordering' section on our website.

ISBN: 978 1 78279 018 1

A CIP catalogue record for this book is available from the British Library.

Design: Stuart Davies

Printed and bound by CPI Group (UK) Ltd, Croydon, CR0 4YY

CONTENTS

Also by Stephen Chong

The Book of Testaments: A practical guide for spiritual realisation, Boolarong Press, Brisbane (2009)

The Music of the Soul: A pathway to a rich and fulfilling life, Sid Harta Publishers, Melbourne (2010)

Foreword

In most societies around the world I would be considered 'old', which, in the West, generally means, 'throw it away and get a new one'. But now I have passed my three score years and ten, with snow upon my roof in this, the winter of my deep content, the extended time has allowed me insights that are rare by today's measure.

My twenty-five thousand days have seen me experience the highest of the highs, in music, sunsets and love, and the lowest of the lows, in child abuse, starvation and brutality. I can view the world from international, national, urban, suburban and rural perspectives.

Once you reach about twenty-five years old, you understand where you sit in the scheme of things with regard to politics, history, science, communication and all the other information that allows us to live and interact in society.

Then, maybe you start to appreciate that there is some other 'stuff' out there. It starts with questioning the world around you, like University students sitting around discussing whether there is a God, how big the universe is and what our place is in the great scheme of things.

Further on still, there are philosophy, art and ethics, and then you have to put all this knowledge and instinct into practice and stand behind your own code of beliefs. As with most things in this life, the world then tries to undermine your values by kicking and pummelling you into the shape of the lowest common denominator: greedy, selfish, dirty and wasteful.

Should you survive that journey, you emerge with a degree of Wisdom, a word that is not used much these days. If your life revolves around McDonald's, Kmart and Facebook, you probably don't have a lot of use for Wisdom.

If, however, you start to be aware of abstract and moral

values, and you question how to put more quality and appreciation into your short life, then *Letters Across Time* is the book for you.

My good friend, Stephen, has a muse that 'marches to the beat of a different drum'. He has worked past the mundane, where admittedly we all have to exist (think of gas, electricity, food, cars and rent/mortgage), but he has gone way beyond that to abstract lessons, fables and stories to illustrate this universal Wisdom – as told through the eyes of a Duck! Now that, my friends, is innovative and inspired!

These ideas are presented as parables: little stories with a message for you to apply to your own life. They are designed to allow you to absorb the lessons his muse presents, into your particular circumstances. It is eminently readable and presents some deep thoughts and questions, but with a light touch.

The language of his muse sometimes appears to be that of a couple of centuries ago, and so it's occasionally quaint and quirky. The substance, however, is very valuable, not immediately in monetary terms, but in enhancing the quality of your present and future life. Those vicissitudes of living that I mentioned before are more easily dealt with, should these lessons be understood. People around you will have more respect for you, and eventually you will become very much your own person. You will mature into an individual of integrity and balance, and one who is trusted and professional, in the sense that you don't need supervision to 'do the right thing'. Your achievements will be greater in depth and easier to attain because of Stephen's concepts.

Stephen has written two other books in the same vein: 'The Book of Testaments' and 'The Music of the Soul'. These, too, come highly recommended. Stephen is a great educator, gentle but forthright, and committed to bettering those people around him, who have possibly lost their way.

We are both 'grey-hairs' and members of Book Creators Circle, where we met, and both of us have a passion for books and for writing.

Stephen's knowledge, together with his ability to communicate, is very rare; so don't miss this one.

People who buy this book will be 'Seekers', people with active, enquiring minds who are looking to answer those questions that are so difficult to frame. They instinctively know that they possess more qualities than others see and will be looking for 'truth and beauty in the Justice of Karma, and the universality of the Spirit'.

In *Letters Across Time* there is a great chance of finding that which you seek.

Chris Shaw
Retired pharmacist, JP and author of 'It's All Relative: Stories to Shorten Your Travel Time'
www.t2d2.com.au
http://www.bookcreatorscircle.com.au/a/Writers/CHRIS_SHAW

Acknowledgements

This book is dedicated to each of my three children, Jaidyn, Brodie & Nicholas – my children are my greatest teachers and a constant reminder of what love is all about. What they have given to my life is a gift beyond all measure.

Behind every good author is an even better editor. I give many thanks to Glyn Davies – of ***Words that Work*** for all his time, wisdom and understanding in making this book a possibility.

Prologue: *The Book of Mysteries*

Throughout *Letters Across Time,* you will read much about another book – the fabled *Book of Mysteries.* I feel it necessary to give those who have not read my previous work an explanation of the origins of this fabled manuscript. Those of you who have read *The Music of the Soul: A pathway to a rich and fulfilling life* will already be aware of how this sacred book came into being … so please bear with me whilst I explain.

The Book of Mysteries was found amongst the ruins of the once vibrant Clanad Pond, by none other than Benjamin Duck, father to Monique, whom you will meet throughout these coming pages. It was Benjamin who, through his vision and resolve, established the library that would house this sacred manuscript.

What is known of the origins of *The Book of Mysteries* is that it was written under the guidance and inspiration of the master duck, Alfred, who was grandfather to Benjamin and father to Jonathon Duck.

The sacred writings within *The Book of Mysteries* have been used by generations of ducks to proclaim the wisdom of the ages, along with many spiritual beliefs and traditions. Like any great works of mysticism and magic, the words of the sacred text will be perceived through the eyes of the beholder. For some, they will be literal, for others they will be mystical, yet for others, they will be *the truth.* Whatever the interpretation, it cannot be denied that the words of this sacred manuscript will be inspirational and change-provoking.

The following is an excerpt from *The* Book of Mysteries, taken from *The Music of the Soul: A pathway to a rich and fulfilling life* (2011):

Love is the basis of everything that is and ever will be. Love cannot die, nor will love be cast aside by the thin veil of death. When you love another, treasure each and every moment that has blessed your togetherness. For, though the moments might be fleeting, they are holy beyond all measure.

Love does not discriminate, nor does love have any bounds or limitations, but as you treasure another, so must you treasure yourself, for truly each of you is an irreplaceable child of God. The love that you would give to another, you must also bestow upon yourself. Treasure who you are and realise that the body, mind and spirit that you are is a joy beyond all knowing for the God that gave you life everlasting.

May the magic and inspiration within *The Book of Mysteries* be a great treasure for you as well.

Introduction

It is a great paradox of life that it generally takes a crisis of some magnitude for us to make significant changes for our betterment. It requires that we receive a 'hammer blow' in order for us to change the things that are demonstrably not working or are decidedly uncomfortable in our life. You know, I've often wondered why this is! Is it because of an in-built resistance to change? Is it that we are fearful of an unknown future? Or, could it be because we are fearful of what we might lose or fail to gain?

When we are faced with this radical crisis, it can lead us down pathways of stress, anxiety, guilt or emotional distress. It may initiate unwanted conditions of poor health, financial challenge or business failure. Whatever the consequences of the crisis, it is a certainty that its purpose is a monumental realignment of how we deal with the world and our inter-personal relationships with the people in it.

I can think of one exemplary circumstance in my own past where the crisis came at the end of a protracted period of having my 'head in the sand', thinking that 'everything would be alright'. At the time, I didn't change, I didn't act to improve the situation. I just thought that by some magical intervention, everything would work out fine. Well, funnily enough, it didn't.

Mind you, the crisis of itself was both a completion and a new beginning. It had a demonstrable way of bringing to an end a situation, which for me, was totally uncomfortable and destructive and not to mention, highly stressful and personally debilitating. It was however also the portent of a new beginning. It was the start of a whole new outlook on life, a brand new vision of the future, and a complete reversal of how I had previously viewed my purpose in life. It was without a doubt the best (and the worst) thing that had ever happened to me. But why, oh why, did it take the crisis for this new outlook to manifest itself?

With the benefit of 20/20 vision, I can see the multitude of opportunities I had to take, some positive action prior to the crisis occurring, to engage and interact at a different level. The changes that I could have made prior to the crisis in my life did in fact occur later, but why did it require such a crisis for me to come to the realisation that they needed to be made? Perhaps it is as Joseph Campbell (2012) says, "Opportunities to find deeper powers come when life seems most challenging".

At its very core, the purpose of *Letters Across Time* is to help you discover, within yourself, the motivation and inspiration to realise your highest potential in life. It will be your ***awakening***. But more than just that, it will be ***enabling***.

It is not enough to say that we should become enlightened or awakened. It is not nearly good enough to say that we should 'shift our consciousness' or 'change our thinking'. These things are important, of course, but what we also need are the 'tools' or the 'skills' to help us achieve these ends.

If you, like me, have days that are full of activity centred around family, children and work commitments then *Letters Across Time* will provide you with some practical everyday ideas that will help you bring about positive and progressive changes in your life.

For those of you that have followed my previous work, *Letters Across Time* contains the continuing story of Benjamin Duck and his descendants, taken from *The Music of the Soul* (2011). Through this, and the many other stories within this book, I will help you discover your fullest potential. Please note though that it is not the purpose of this book to *tell* you anything. Rather, it will be for you to *discover* within yourself, the greatest version of the grandest vision of who you really are. Once you embark on that process of discovery the practical, everyday suggestions and ideas that are contained within the book, will provide you with the enabling tools to see your fullest potential come to realisation. In other words, the book will take you on a great journey – but your destination is for you alone to make manifest.

When we go on this journey, you and I, we will be traversing some topics that, at a minimum will be very interesting, but at some other level, may indeed be confronting or uncomfortable. We will discuss grief, sorrow and loneliness. We will traverse issues of morality and systems of belief. Some of the stories may even elicit the prospect of challenging the current way you view life and the way you currently view yourself, and others.

So, is this a life-changing book? Well, only if you desire it to be so. Only if you are ready, willing and able (see Chapter 5) to heed that little voice in your ear, that feeling in your 'gut' that says, "This isn't working - this isn't what I'm about – this is not helping me to reach my fullest potential". Then you will know you are ready. Then, you will feel the inspiration and motivation to make the essential changes in your life that will help you realise your fullest potential.

Oh, and I must tell you about stories and how they work, for this book is full of stories.

Parables and stories enable us to choose our own level of understanding and examine our personal motives. Each story and parable will have its own meaning and context for you, given where you are on your particular life journey. What this means is that you have made a critical connection with the story's significance from your current perspective and point of reference. I urge you to consider the different levels of understanding when reading these parables and stories.

The first level of understanding is the *literal* level – the most obvious. The second is *allegorical;* in that the story illustrates or touches on some other meaning, not just its outward form. At a deeper *metaphysical* level, the story may illustrate a universal law, or principle. Fourthly, the story or parable may be understood on a *mystical* level - where it touches the heart so deeply that your particular TRUTH is deeply experienced.

Let these stories work their magic for you and let them inspire you to achieve great things in your life. Once they work their magic, use this knowledge as your inspiration and motivation. Indeed, you could read the stories again and again, each time extracting a different message or meaning. This is your process of discovery.

Come along with me now. Let's really enjoy the journey, a journey of discovery - *the realisation of your fullest potential* - with an irresistible sense of purpose.

It is as Nelson Mandela said in his inaugural speech (1994), "Your playing small doesn't serve this world."

Chapter 1

Grief is natural, suffering is a judgement

… the duck story recommences:

For Monique, the death of her father came as monumental a blow to her sense of self, of a kind she had never before encountered in her short life. She was blooming into womanhood from the turbulence of her teenage years, but the loss of her father engulfed her in a grief as profound as the deepest mire. It was as if her *raison d'être* had been severed and her lifeline of support and counsel had abruptly ceased to exist.

There were many who came to the funeral of course, because Benjamin was the founding father of the community's library. The library had become an icon of learning and knowledge throughout the duck world. Over the years, many wise and learned figures had traversed the hallowed halls and sought information amongst the thousands of tomes that graced the now multitudinous rooms and caverns of the library's labyrinths.

It was Benjamin who had been the principle driver of the project, dating right back to his original discovery of the famed and renowned *Book of Mysteries* that graced the library and represented the principal and most treasured manuscript of the library's vast collection. This tome, along with all of the other valuable volumes, now represented a vast expanse of knowledge derived from much of the known world.

Indeed, even in the short time since Benjamin's death, many reports, articles and glossaries had been compiled identifying him as a hero to the nation, and a fine example of what one single duck could achieve in a lifetime that was markedly short in the overall scheme of things.

It was at the funeral of her father, some two weeks after his passing, that Monique really saw the vastness of the influence that her father had had on the duck world. The mourners came, not just in their hundreds, but most assuredly in their thousands. There were politicians, academics, community elders, teachers and scholars from all parts of the globe. All came to pay homage to the person that Benjamin had been and to recognise the work he had done, as well as to pledge further support and energy to the library that had been his unique vision and motivation.

For Monique, this period was a whirlwind of encounters with people she did not know. She was eternally being embraced with good wishes and kindnesses from learned dignitaries and lay-ducks alike, with gifts, pledges and mementos. The support and love from this community of ducks can only be described as remarkable. It demonstrated the sheer magnitude of love that resides in the heart of each individual.

Yet, all of this activity and loving kindness could not properly disguise the profound feeling of loss and pain Monique was enduring in the quiet of her heart, particularly when the lights were turned off at night and the stillness of her room replaced the frenzied activity of the daylight hours.

She cried, she lamented to her God, and at the deepest point of despair, she even considered ending her own life prematurely, just to gain relief from her suffering. But fortunately, these disturbances of mind did not last more than fleeting seconds before she released her aberrant thoughts to the universe and her God.

She was alone. There was no one else in her family. Her mother had passed away many moons ago and Monique was the sole offspring of the relationship between Benjamin and his wife Nadene. Eventually, after some days, the crowds that attended the funeral returned to their homes and their everyday tasks.

Monique returned to her job as *chargé d'affaires* for the library and was immediately engulfed in a maelstrom of activity that filled her every waking moment – but her life was empty! It was as if she was operating out of someone else's body, as if the tasks and activities she undertook were hollow and without purpose.

Yes, things got done, but her heart was an empty space, a black hole, from which nothing that entered could identifiably return.

A Story: A Brother's Love

It was a fine, sunny day and the master was enjoying the serenity of his walk amongst the garden of flowers and native bushes. As he wandered and gazed, he noted that the variety of scents from the assorted flora were as an elixir for a tired soul. Interrupting his reverie, his appointed novice came up to him in supplication and distress.

'What ails you my son?' said the master.

'Master, over these past weeks I have been sorely distressed for the loss of my brother. As you know, he was killed in a tragic accident that none on this earth could have foreseen or prevented. Truly, I miss him so and my heart feels ready to burst for the suffering I endure.'

The Master pondered the distress of his novice with great compassion. Then, after some moments, he bade the novice to sit on the rock by the corner of the garden bed.

'What do you hear?' enquired the master to the novice.

'Master, I hear the chirping of the birds as they take flight between the trees. I hear the buzzing of the bees as they seek joy from the flowers.'

'This is so,' said the master, 'and what do you now feel?'

'I feel momentarily at peace from the turmoil of my mind in its grief for the loss of my brother.'

'This peace, can you not experience it from this time here on?' enquired the master.

'But master, my mind keeps returning to the things I wish I had said to my brother, to the many things we should have done as brothers, as well as the many times I was cruel and nasty to him.'

'My son, death is a mystery, but what I do know is that life ends naturally when we have learned everything we needed to learn in this lifetime. Do you not think your brother loves you unconditionally from his place now in heaven's eternity and alongside God the Almighty? Just as you love him?'

'Yes master, but I miss him so much and my suffering is great,' exclaimed the novice.

'That you miss and grieve for your brother is a reflection of the great love you have for him, and undoubtedly you always will. Yet, I say to you that, as with the birds and the bees in this flower garden, the love of mother earth for its treasured beings does not diminish for those of us that remain earth-bound. Therefore, seek peace in the joy to be found in the essence of the flowers and the trees. Know that your brother's love for you remains total and unconditional and is yours to find in the silence of a quiet mind and loving heart. Let your love for him be a beacon for all the remaining days of your time here on earth, and from the grief that you feel, seek only that which is your highest purpose, with thoughts of peace and love for all others.'

Good Grief:

According to Soygal Rinpoche, (1992), "People who are grieving go through a kind of death. Just like a person who is actually dying, they need to know that the disturbing emotions they feel are natural."

The Duck story continues:

The air on this particular evening was more chilled than was normally the case for this time of year. Monique had returned home from her daily travails only to find a house in darkness and devoid of warmth and whilst she busied herself to light a fire, it did little to remove the pallid feel of depression that engulfed her.

Standing in the middle of the lounge room, she at once began to cry. Great tears of lament and grief shook her diminutive body. It was as if the sorrows of a lifetime had risen to overwhelm this tender and youthful soul. What was she to do now? What purpose did life hold for her, now that both of her parents were dead? For many moments it did indeed seem as if there was no end to the grief that she felt so abjectly.

As the tears rolled unabated down her visage, she heard a faint knocking, barely audible above the sound of her sobbing. Someone, it seemed, was knocking at her door. Quickly, with the sleeve of her cloak, she wiped the tears from her cheeks and wondering who would venture to her doorstep at this hour and in this frigid cold, she went down the hallway to open the door to the unexpected visitor.

With feelings of dread and foreboding at this intrusion, Monique opened the door, but only a fraction so that she could espy who was stationed on her porch. To her surprise, what she saw was a bedraggled, scruffy young duck who was shivering in the chilled night air.

'Who are you and what do you want?' was the terse enquiry to the dishevelled visitor.

'I'm here because I'm meant to be here,' was the shivered, but none the less assertive reply from the visitor.

'What do you mean? Speak plainly, or I'll cast you away and call the police to have you removed.'

'I'm here because you are in dire need of comfort and solace. It is this call that I have heard, and I have come to offer you the cheer of an open ear and heart.'

'Come in then, but be warned if you dare attempt anything untoward I'll ensure that your stay in my home will be uncomfortable and demonstrably unwise,' said a wary Monique.

As the visitor shook the cold wind from his feathers and stood beside the now blazing fire to put warmth back into his bones, Monique said, 'What is your name and where did you come from?'

'I am known as Gabriel, but you would know of me as the nephew of your father's old mentor, Mandrake. As you know, your late father and Mandrake were very close colleagues for many years and my uncle was associated with many of the ventures that your father undertook over the years.'

Monique visibly relaxed at these words and proceeded to offer her guest the warmth of a beverage and the sustenance of a bowl of warm stew that she had previously prepared for dinner. After Gabriel had taken his fill and was feeling much more invigorated, he was asked the purpose of his visit.

'In my world,' stated Gabriel, 'when we lose a treasured loved one, it is vital that we help that person through their loss. The feelings of loss, sadness, anger and denial are all a part of the grieving process. All these feelings are of great poignancy. One should not be left to fend on one's own when these powerful emotions come to visit. It is for this reason that I am here and, when you are ready, you may allow these feelings to emerge from within, so they no longer cause you distress and anguish.'

'But why?' said Monique. 'How did you know that I have need of such generosity of spirit?'

'Know?' exclaimed Gabriel, 'How does the bee know when to seek the flower?'

The hours passed slowly that night and many tears cascaded down Monique's face. She relived many of the pleasant days spent in the company of her parents and rejoiced in the multitude of adventures and triumphs that they had shared as a family. Then, at the point where there were no more tears, Gabriel said to her, 'With the loving grace of your mother and father always within your heart, how will you now be in your life?'

'What do you mean, how will I be in my life?' asked a bemused Monique.

'From this moment forward you have the choice of being the grandest version of the greatest vision that you can aspire to for yourself,' stated Gabriel. 'You can choose to *be* sad, depressed and angry, or you can choose to *be* loving, peaceful and vibrant, just as your parents knew you and would want you to be in all the days to come.'

At these words, Monique felt a peace that had eluded her for many weeks past. She closed her eyes, and descended into a profound slumber in which her troubled soul was able to reconnect with the wider expanses of the universe.

In the morning, as she awoke, the fire was ablaze with a glowing warmth and the intoxicating smell of freshly ground coffee and baking bread was emanating from the kitchenette of her small abode.

She was not surprised to find Gabriel busying himself with the morning breakfast tasks. He smiled his greetings with some trepidation given the assumptions he had made about using her kitchen; then he bade Monique sit at the table and partake of the morning's fare.

The meal was conducted mostly in silence, but not a silence borne of embarrassment or discomfort; rather the silence was one of a gentle peace and serenity that emanated from both of the souls present. After they had broken fast and made busy with the chores of cleaning up and putting away, Gabriel took Monique gently by the hand and bade her to walk outside to the small garden area that surrounded her humble dwelling. It was here that he described the nature of grief. In a kind and gentle manner he explained,

'When grief casts its shadow upon you, it is important for you to know that what you feel is a reflection of your deepest love for those that have departed. It is your heart's anguish that cries out for that which can be no more on this physical plane. In the midst of your sorrow, you will feel anger, denial, sorrow and blame. You will experience each of these in cycles until your grief has been fully expressed, for grief unexpressed remains undissolved. When that time arrives, however, you will come to accept fully, in love and grace, that which has occurred. As a beginning to this journey, I ask you to take this pen and paper and write down that which is in your heart as a letter to your dearly departed father'.

This is what Monique did. She wrote:

You held my hand through all of my fears,
When I cried it was upon your shoulder,
It was your words that soothed my pain,
Your strength that chased away my darkness.
How can you expect me to carry on now that you are no longer here?
What do you expect me to do?
Where do I now turn when my fears overtake me?
You could have told me how it would be without you,
I feel your presence even now, but you are not here,
I always knew you'd go, but why does it have to be so hard,
Time passes in your absence, but each moment is a void,
You are still with me, but I'm still alone.
Come back and dry my tears, for each moment is like an eternity
This pain is very real,
Life can no longer be the same, how can it be?
There has been too much that time cannot erase,
Now that you are gone, do you see my tears?
But finally, I realise, I am your child,
All of your love will be with me forever and eternity,
I will love you each and every moment, and I will go on,
By grace will I take each next step of my life,
For I know your love and it will never diminish,
But I will miss you ever till we are reunited beyond the veil.

According to Ricard (2003),

> When it (death) comes along, it is all the more shocking because we are unprepared for it. Meanwhile life has been slipping away day after day, and if we have not learned to find meaning in its every passing moment, all it has meant to us is a waste of time.

Elizabeth Kubler-Ross in her book, *The Wheel of Life: A Memoir of Living and Dying* (1997), described the various stages of the death and dying process as:

- Shock & denial
- Rage & anger
- Grief & pain
- Bargaining (with God)
- Depression (... why me?)

Then finally, she said that those who grieve,

> Experience withdrawal into themselves for a bit, separating themselves from others while hopefully reaching a stage of peace and acceptance (not resignation which occurs when tears and anger are not shared).

... we return to Monique's story

Many nights of anguish passed by, but under Gabriel's compassionate gaze, Monique was able to express the depth of her grief. Of particular interest, on one of these troubled nights, she was railing against her God! Indeed, for such a mild-mannered and serene duck, the invective of rage and torment was something to behold. Monique, as she told the story many times later, had determined to have a real good talking to God. She related the story something like this:

'If you are such an omnipotent being, why did my parents have to die? Couldn't you do something in all your high and mightiness? My parents were the most beautiful of beings, why did they have to die so young yet with so much to do? And what now of me, what am I going to do? I've got no family. What in the hell am I supposed to do now? You've taken away the only family and loved-ones I've ever known! You sit up there on your high and mighty throne and expect us mere mortals to figure it all out for ourselves. Not to mention the trials and tribulations you put my father through with that financial scandal … why didn't you do something? It's no wonder that The Bible tells us to "have faith", because we have to … we don't hear from you!'

As you can imagine the tears of lament were many for Monique this very night, and in between her sobs and outpourings, the only sound she could hear was the constant ticking of the grandfather clock that her father had given her on her last birthday, and that stood proudly in the corner of the room.

Some two nights later, in a fit of desperation to ease her suffering, Monique decided to visit the pond's library and once there, she made her way directly to the room that housed the treasured *Book of Mysteries* that was the origin and founding book of the entire library's collection.

Everything was quiet. The visiting crowds of the day had all gone, and she determinedly approached the room that held the sacred book. As she approached the doorway, she could hear a faint rustling of wind and what sounded like pages of the book being shuffled, although she thought that maybe it was just her senses playing tricks on her.

As she neared the sacred tome, the feathers on the nape of her neck rose with the sensation of a higher presence in the room. She looked around between the light and the shadows, but could see no other presence. Yet the feeling of a grand spirit being present was powerful beyond measure. Just for a moment she closed her eyes and said a silent prayer to the God she had so derided just the previous evening.

She asked openly, 'God are you here?'

The reply did not come in words, but more as a feeling or a sensation. The answer she received was, 'Yes, in truth, I have never left you.'

Monique was at first startled, but then accepting of the events as they were unfolding, she asked, 'Why did you not answer me the previous night when I was in such pain and need?'

'I did,' was the answer she received, 'but you were not listening.'

Now, feeling a little more at ease with the conversation, she said, 'What now is to become of me, what am I to do with my life now that my parents are gone?'

'Firstly,' was the reply, 'your parents are both here with me – in what you call heaven, but I simply refer to it as home. They are both blissful and want you to know that they are together in a place beyond happiness. Their spirits are united as one pure essence that nothing could ever break asunder. They send you their limitless love and want you to know that you merely have to think of them and they will be by your side and in your heart - in a time shorter than a heartbeat.'

'As for you, with all the anguish you expressed to me the other eve, you must know that I will never, ever leave you. In truth, I cannot, for you and I are one.'

'But how can I know this, what do I have to do?' asked Monique.

'Do? You do not have to do anything. Rather, in the forthcoming days, the unfolding of your life's purpose will be the catalyst for you to experience the greatest version of the grandest vision of who you really are. Ask yourself now the question – "if I were to die tomorrow, what would I truly most regret?"'

Monique pondered this question deeply, then replied, 'I would regret not having extended the vision of my father and made people realise the grand potential of his library. It is such that all of the world may benefit from the knowledge and learning to be found here. I would also regret not finding someone to share my life's journey with and perhaps even starting a family of my own.'

'Then so be it,' came the reply, 'you have with you the beginnings of a grand adventure, and … by the way, I have opened *The Book of Mysteries* to the page that you most need to read.'

Monique then turned her attention to the page that lay open from the book. It read:

Never, ever be afraid, I am your God Almighty. I am with you always, even unto the end of time. My love for you is eternal, as you are my treasured child, a star that burns bright in the night sky. Whatever you do, wherever you go – I am with you. You need only seek me in the silence of your heart.

Chapter 2

Every person has a gift – find it, use it.

A story: The Majesty of an Urchin

A bedraggled young urchin was found one morning knocking on the door of the monastery. The day was extremely cold, for the chill of the west wind carved into everything it touched. The young urchin could not have been more than ten years old. His clothes were threadbare and torn, and it looked as if he had not had a square meal for many weeks. His matted hair, filthy visage and sunken cheeks even made it appear that he was not of sound mind.

Yet, as the monk opened the large oak door of the monastery, he felt an immediate sense of compassion for the young urchin, and bade him to enter the sacred sanctuary. The first thing that the kind monk did was to take the boy to the kitchen, where he was given a bowl of refreshing broth and bread to satisfy his hunger. The speed with which the fare was devoured was of itself a miracle to behold. It was no sooner on the table than it was gone, into the ravenous mouth that had not tasted such sustenance for many a day. The boy was then taken to the bathing area and allowed to wash away the grime of many weeks of foraging and rough living. Subsequently, given a clean set of robes to wear, he came to resemble a rejuvenated young human being.

The attending monk then bade the young man to sit in the nearby courtyard and await further instructions as to his wellbeing. Some minutes later, the master Abbott of the monastery came to seek the boy's attention and talk with him about his story. Alas however, the Abbott found the young charge curled into a ball, sound asleep on the cobblestones of the courtyard - in such a sound sleep that only the dead were more at peace.

The Abbott, with firm tenderness, took the boy in his arms and lifted him into the nearest lodgings where he could sleep undisturbed until he was well rested and had recovered strength in his diminutive body. Some twenty-four hours later the Abbott was informed that the young lad had awakened and had broken his fast with yet another substantial repast. The Abbott instructed the attending monk to bring the boy to the sacred meditation hall where he could commence his inquiries in the hope of uncovering the boy's history.

As the master Abbott sat upon his meditation mat, he bade the young boy to come and sit on the mat placed in front of him. The master observed that the young man, although diminutive and in obvious awe of the splendour of the sacred hall, was yet unafraid appearing quite at ease even in the face of such an imposing figure as the master of the monastery.

'Young man,' began the Abbott, 'know that you are safe within the walls of this institution. No harm will befall you, but in order for us to tend to your needs, we need to know the story of who you are and whence you have come.'

The young boy told the Abbott his name. It was Joshua … he didn't know his second name and as he told his story, the master became more and more aghast at the plight of the young man. The boy had endured deprivations beyond any human expectation for one so young. For as long as the young lad could remember he'd been summarily beaten by his abusive mother. He was made to toil in the fields, by his father, from dawn until dusk each day and, while his parents ate decent fare almost every day, he was made to survive merely on the scraps and remains from the table. He told the Abbott how, unlike other children, he was never sent to school, but had managed to learn the rudiments of reading and writing from the books and literature he scavenged from a nearby refuse heap. The young boy confirmed his story by showing the Abbott the welt marks that criss-crossed his back and his legs. He then described how he had run away from this abuse, and with nowhere else to go, had made his way many a mile, to the doorstep of the monastery.

The Abbott, with great compassion and understanding, said to the young man, 'Your body is bruised from your many beatings – but these, in time will heal. Given time, your body will recover its strength and you will grow into a healthy and strong man. But tell me young man, what of your spirit? How do you feel in your heart about what has occurred to you in your life?'

The young lad pondered the Abbott's question for some moments, and then said in reply, 'Master, my heart is full of gratitude for the experiences I have endured in my life for, in truth, without these experiences, harsh as they have been, I would not now be sitting here in your presence.'

The master was amazed at the wisdom of these words from a person so young, and while he did not allow his inner thoughts to show on his face, he said to the young man, 'My son, I see that you have a wisdom beyond your years and it is with an open heart that I offer you the opportunity to stay in the monastery as a novice. God willing, one day, this will lead you to become a master monk. But be aware, this journey will not be one of pleasure or ease. Rather, it will be one of much hardship and trials of the spirit.'

'Master, these trials can be no more arduous than many I have already encountered and even if I should fail, it will have been a journey of joy and amazement that will be a wonder in itself. I will learn my lessons well and apply myself diligently to the task of learning.'

'Welcome then, my son, to this humble monastery, and may God be your guide for all of the days that you spend amongst our fold.'

So it was that the young man undertook the journey of learning, both for his regular schooling and for his spiritual enlightenment. Many years later Joshua assumed the title of master of the Abbey, after the current master had passed on. Right throughout his life, he remained ever thankful for the experiences he had as a youth and the grand opportunity to join the monastery that the master Abbott had so generously bestowed upon him in his time of need.

Gratitude - the great enabler

It would be quite a feat of personal achievement to be able to declare that we are free from any regrets or guilt about past experiences in our life. Or, that there are events that occurred which, with the benefit of hindsight, could have been handled in a much more proficient manner. Indeed, we can look back on particular instances in our life when we know that decisions made and actions taken have precipitated major 'changes in direction' and have propelled us along a particular pathway. Our vision in hindsight of these events is of course 20/20 and so we perceive the 'error of our ways', or know 'how we'd do it differently next time'.

Interestingly, Walsch, N.D. (2006), said that, "Every act is an act of self-definition." Perhaps I might phrase this idea in a different way.

> *Our purpose in life is to evolve, to realise who we really are – to define our true purpose. We do this via life's experiences. The quickest means then, to evolve, is to be thankful for the experiences that we have in life.*

... and we return to the ducks.

Following the enlightening experiences with her new friend and colleague, Gabriel, it was with renewed vigour and energy that Monique applied herself to her role as *chargé d'affaires* within the community's world-renowned library. In fact, it was only six months later that the library's board of management had more than enough reasons to promote her to the role of General

Manager. It was a most prestigious role, both within the library, and, more broadly, within the pond's community of ducks; it had grown substantially as a result of the library's renown throughout the duck world. In truth, it seemed quite appropriate that Monique should assume such a role. Her work was recognised to be of exceptionally high quality, as was her previous experience as an investigative journalist. Many remembered that she was responsible for uncovering the culprit behind the library's financial scandal a couple of years before. These memories were still fresh in the minds of many who had been involved in that sorry saga.

Monique, of course, plunged into her new role with an earnestness and gusto that would bring a smile to the face of any expectant shareholder. For many months she managed and directed the numerous facets of the library's administration, including it must be said, the challenges of dealing with the wide variety of interest groups and stakeholders that had an investment in it.

One night, some six months after taking up her new role, Monique, returned home in the early evening and opened the door of her living room, only to feel that sixth sense that something was wrong, something was different. She looked around the room, but nothing seemed out of place. Nothing was missing that she could put her finger on. Then, all of a sudden, she realised what it was. Her constant companion in this room for many years had been the grandfather clock that her father had given her numerous moons ago ticking away in the background. It was like the sound you don't hear even when you hear it … it was always there, but now it had stopped.

She noticed that the pendulum had stopped swinging. This of itself was quite amazing for the clock had never missed a beat for as long it had been in the family's possession. Although she did not consider herself mechanically minded, she opened the door of the clock in an effort to find the cause of the problem.

Rummaging around amongst things mechanical was, to be sure, not a forte of our intrepid investigative journalist, but as she was foraging around in the back crevice of the clock, her hand felt something odd, something certainly out of place. It felt a bit like plastic wrapping, and with her curiosity now at its peak, she removed the package from its plastic cover. She thought at first that it might only be some infernal instructions about the operation and mechanics of the offending timepiece, and probably in some foreign language at that. She opened the plastic and discovered to her absolute amazement, an envelope with her name hand-written on the front. 'What on earth ...?' she said to no one in particular.

The opened envelope revealed a letter, addressed to her and sent from none other than her late great grandfather, Alfred, the wise seer of his age and author of *The Book of Mysteries*. Monique's hands began to tremble as she read the epistle, for she knew this to be something momentous, knowing as she did that the stories of her late, great grandfather were often life changing. This is what she read:

> Dearest Monique,
> I am your great grandfather, Alfred. Like your father before you, I know of you through what you would call 'the wisdom of the ages'. This wisdom has its foundation in love. Love has the ability to traverse the folds of time to reveal things that only love can declare.
>
> While you are reading this letter, you should know that both your mother and father are here with me in heaven. You already know that both your parents are joyous, with unconditional love, and are proud of you beyond measure ... and so am I. Already in your young life you have achieved many things, but your journey so far has been short. Much remains for you to accomplish in your lifetime.
>
> All of the good books that have traversed the ages, with all

of the wisdom they contain, have explained that there is only one God – He that is the all in all, and that all is love. Yet, I say to you, that as you come to realise this love, your pathway to experience who you really are is fraught with many challenges, pitfalls and regrets. Yet, none of these things should ever be considered a failure. In the eyes of God, you cannot fail – for pure love cannot abide such judgement. In truth, it is your true spirit that brings forth all of life's experiences so that you may within this lifetime truly realise who you are and manifest the highest version of your greatest vision of yourself.

Therefore, I say to you that with all of your heart and all of your soul – be thankful. Be thankful for all the experiences that life brings your way. Do not give in to guilt, anger or regret. These limit your true potential within the precious moments of time that are available to you. The wise amongst you say that, you will never fly if you are tied to the rocks of guilt, anger and regret.

Be grateful for all of your experiences. Give thanks to God for their manifestation and never, ever be afraid – but I know that you have already learned this lesson.

In the many challenging days to come, I urge you to commune with your God, thankful for the experiences that will come to your door. Seek counsel and the answer to your questions in the silence of your heart, for this is where your true self resides.

It was *The Book of Mysteries* from which this great adventure across time sprang and it will be the good book that ensures the closure of the story. Seek always to guard its treasures, for many will seek its power and majesty for their own limited self-interested purposes – but that is not the purpose of *The Book of Mysteries*. It is not a book for some, but for all who have eyes to read, ears to hear and a heart that is open to the grace within.

My dearest Monique, in all that you do, be steadfast and purposeful, but most of all know that love is the basis of all things that ever have been and ever will be. It is I, Alfred, your great grandfather, who wishes you love, but what I wish for, you already have.

Yours truly,
Alfred

A Story: The Greatness of Gratitude

'Grand Master,' came the entreaty from his young apprentice, 'I have heard you speak much of 'being grateful', but for all of my want of trying, I cannot let go of my anger towards my mother. She treated me so badly for so many years. As you know, she was abusive and unstable, and made my youth a journey of much unhappiness.'

'My son, that you should feel the intensity of these emotions is a natural part of the human condition. It is important not to berate yourself, nor consider yourself unworthy in any way for having these feelings. Merely acknowledge the presence of these powerful memories and emotions. Just observe them as you would a spectator at a game of sport - but do not attach to them.'

Then the Grand Master said, 'Come with me, I want to show you something.' The master and the apprentice then walked a short distance to a wishing well in the centre of the village. As both the master and the apprentice peered into the depths of the well, the master said, 'What do those coins at the bottom of the well represent?'

'Master, each coin represents somebody's wish for something better in their lives. They desire that something be fixed or brought to them that will make life a little more pleasant.'

'This is quite so,' said the Master, 'but why do they believe, that by casting coins into a pool of water, their desires will be made manifest?'

'I guess this is because they do not firmly believe in the grace of God. They feel He must be cajoled with coin, so they can be provided with what they need.'

'This is so, young apprentice, but the real reason is that they do not give thanks for the many gifts that have been bestowed upon them.'

'But master,' interrupted the apprentice, 'many of these people have little in the way of possessions. They are poor and impoverished, some are sick from maladies, or cast upon by evil doers wishing to do them harm.'

'Your observations are quite poignant, young apprentice. Just like you, many of these people have traversed a lifetime of experiences that would be considered harsh, challenging and demanding, but to view these experiences through the prism of hatred, malice or malcontent, suffices only to make them more real. It is like feeding a wolf that threatens to devour you.'

'But master, what do I need to do to rid myself of these unwanted legacies?'

'Do?' said the master. 'You need not 'do' anything! You simply need to 'be' … be grateful.'

'But master, I don't understand.'

'My son, each morning, as you arise, say unto yourself, 'Today I will be grateful, peaceful and loving'. Repeat this same mantra each time an unwanted thought about a past experience enters your mind. Do this for as long as your mind continues to tie you to the past. This 'state of being' will liberate you from the shackles of guilt and regret. It will set you free to realise your grand purpose while you are in this body – a purpose that will help you realise who you really are.'

'Master,' said the young apprentice, 'from the bottom of my heart - thank you'.

A radio interview:

I was listening to the radio this morning, while driving my car to a business engagement. The story on the radio struck me as extremely pertinent given the topic of our current discussion.

A man related his life experience about his prowess at and love of playing the flute as a teenager. His playing the flute gave him a great deal of joy and, indeed, he was passionate about all things musical. Given his significant skill with the flute, he was entered, by his father, into a state-wide competition. He achieved a result of 97 out of 100, a result not previously achieved by any competitor throughout the history of the competition. When the judges declared the result, the boy's father proceeded to rip up the scorecard and deride the judges.

'That result was a waste of three marks,' he said. 'You've got to try harder next time.'

Because of this experience, even fourteen years later, the young man never again picked up a flute (or any other musical instrument), even though he still had a keen love and gift for music.

What a burden this young man carried! What a waste of an obviously prodigious, God-given talent!

According to Seligman, M.E.P. (2002), "You can't hurt the perpetrator by not forgiving, but you can set yourself free by forgiving."

Elisabeth Kubler-Ross (1997), wrote about her experience of meeting a young Jewess, named Golda, just after the second-world war. She wrote:

> *(This) gorgeous young girl, had been the last person they tried to squeeze in before closing the door and turning on the gas. By some miracle, by some divine intervention, the door would not close with her in there. It was too crowded. She was taken out of the extermination room and, since she had been listed on the 'death list', she was presumed dead and was never ever again called. Thanks to an unusual oversight, her life was spared.*

This story is remarkable in and of itself, but Golda, despite the trauma, deprivations and horror of these experiences said, after her liberation,

> *Like Hitler, if I used my life, which was spared, to sow the seeds of hatred, I would not be any different to him. The only way we can find peace is to let the past be the past.*

It was Walsch, N.D. (1999) who said:

> *Accepting something does not mean refusing to change it. In fact, the opposite is true. You cannot change that which you do not accept – in yourself especially, and outside of yourself as well ... To accept something is not to agree with it. It is simply to embrace it, whether you agree with it or not.*

... and back to the pond.

For many days after her profound experience with her great grandfather's letter, Monique walked around in a kind of mystic haze. She felt light headed and not a little overwhelmed by the momentousness of the experience. It boggled her logical and practical mind. She wondered how her great grandfather even knew of her existence, let alone the way he delivered his epistle.

Anyway, despite the fact that her analytical mind could not grasp the profundity of the experience, she accepted with a mix of gratitude and awe, the reality of the occurrence. Then there was also the wonder she felt for her part in the stage play that was surely about to unfold around *The Book of Mysteries*.

Some days later, she was working on the operational aspects of a project that would entail none other than a visit by the Prime Minister of the country, Sir Albert Duckworth, to their library and humble duck community. As you can imagine, this would be akin to a 'once in a lifetime experience', not only for Monique herself, but also for the many other ducks in the pond's community. It was mid-morning when Monique's personal assistant came running into her office. The assistant's face was flushed red and her breathing came in laboured gasps that barely allowed her to express a word.

'Judy, what on earth is it? Are you okay? Is everything alright?' enquired Monique with concern.

'Madam, the book ... the book is missing,' stammered Judy between laboured gasps.

'What on earth are you talking about? Slow down, what book is missing?'

'*The Book of Mysteries*, our treasure, is gone. It's not in its rightful place and nobody knows where it is.'

Monique's jaw went slack and the colour drained from her cheeks. 'How in God's name did this happen? What about all the security cameras we've installed and the security guards? Surely they know something.'

Monique darted over to the room where the treasured book was usually held. When she arrived, she saw all the assembled security personnel wandering around in search of the sacred tome.

'You there,' pointing to the officer in charge, 'would you mind telling me what in God's name is going on here?'

In a trembling voice, the chief of security said, 'Madam, no one knows where the book has gone. When my officers did their usual rounds, everything was normal. But when Officer Jordan,' now pointing to the young security guard over in the corner, 'was checking in the room he discovered that the book was missing.'

'Have you checked the security footage from the cameras?' asked Monique.

'Yes, but there seems to be some discrepancy with the timing,' said Jordan.

Now Monique was as angry as she had ever been in her life, and she stood toe-to-toe with her chief of security. 'What do you mean - some discrepancy with the timing?'

Beads of sweat began to appear on the security officer's brow as he explained that while the tapes showed an undisturbed area surrounding the treasured book, the timing of the video displayed a missing five minutes that could not be explained. It was as if someone had tampered with the tapes to record an uninterrupted sequence of events, but had failed to put together the correct time sequence so as to ensure the tampering would not be discovered.

'You mean to tell me,' continued Monique, 'that someone has deliberately altered the tapes to make it look as if nothing has happened?'

'Yes, that is exactly as it appears, madam,' said the exasperated security manager.

The remainder of the day, for Monique, became a whirlwind of interviews both with the attending police and the intrusive media pack with their incessant enquiries as to the events leading up to the theft of the sacred tome. It was well into the late hours of the evening before Monique was finally able to seek refuge in the quiet of her abode. But her heart trembled with the pain of ultimate responsibility. Her sleep was interrupted with non-stop thoughts of how this calamity had happened and what she should now do to see to the book's safe return.

Chapter 3

We are moral creatures, but whose morality do we serve?

It was only some thirty or forty years ago that babies born to unwed mothers in our society were automatically given up for adoption and the mothers shunned and ostracised from the society from which they so badly needed support. Often, these unwed mothers were disenfranchised from their families and cast aside by the government of the day. Mothers were separated from their children by virtue of their marital status – not their familial stability, maternal capability or any other personal attributes. Yet, over this same period we were taught, as we continue to be taught, to behave according to the maxim … "Love thy neighbour as thyself". Today, unwed mothers contribute a significant proportion of the births within our Western societies, and nowadays, are recognised and supported by governments through packages of monetary assistance and institutional support services. The passage of time - and not much time at that - has seen a dramatic change in the moral values of our society. Moral imperatives, that some forty years ago were considered 'the right thing to do', have been altered, sometimes drastically.

The conundrum then with moral values is that they change from time to time, from generation to generation, and most certainly differ according to cultures, countries, and even localities across the globe. In other words, morals and values are very subjective.

The Oxford English Dictionary defines *morality* as, "the degree of conformity of an idea, practice, etc. to moral principles." Contra wise, the Oxford English Dictionary defines *immorality* as, "not conforming to accepted standards of morality (esp. in sexual matters)". The question is however, not what morality is, but rather, *who* defines morality? Is it our parents? Is it our government, through the creation and implementation of laws through its legislature? Is it our religious leaders, by virtue of their doctrines and interpretations of sacred and ancient texts? Or perhaps it is our academics of high esteem and ethical standing. Behaviours that are described as immoral are those that violate some 'code' or 'law' of society that has been written or enacted, or more descriptively that the society has deemed God or their chosen Deity to have decreed.

In his book, *Conversations with God: an Uncommon Dialogue*, Walsch, (1998), stated that, "No matter is inconsequential. There is a consequence to everything. The consequence is who and what you are."

This, in reality, provides us with considerations of morality based on self-interest – a certain recipe for anarchy and self-destruction, given our limited definition of the self. A myopic view of self at that! A myopic view of 'self' is ME. A more expansive view of self may be, MY FAMILY. An even more expansive view of 'self' may be MY GROUP, e.g. my religious affiliation or community group, my race, my ethnicity or my culture. We might even expand this further to encompass, MY NATIONALITY.

These definitions of self, however, are self-limiting. They create a separation between those whom we define as 'within the self' and all those others who are excluded from such a definition. If, for example, we consider the self as those within our religious community – or those who believe in a particular faith, then those outside of this faith, or 'the non-believers' are separated and defined by their differences. In the event of some disagreement or difference of opinion, it becomes far easier to consider these people and their beliefs as 'wrong' simply because they have been defined as different, or separated from 'the true believers'.

But if we truly embrace a whole and complete definition of

the self as ALL OTHERS or AS ONE WITH ALL OTHERS, then the morality of self interest becomes 'Do unto others, as you would do to yourself' and 'That which you would not do to yourself, do not do unto others'.

But how, indeed, do we experience this sense of ONENESS. It is not something that we can call upon on demand. The many great teachers over the ages have described their oneness and unity with all sentient beings. But how can we 'mere mortals' even begin to experience this oneness, when ever since we were born, we have been taught to recognise and develop our 'sense of self'.

For example, Kuik, A. (2011) states:

When I'm in a conversation with someone, if I find that I'm thinking about how I'm going to respond ... I could turn my attention fully to what they were saying, with the intention of really understanding their perspective.

She continues:

If I often make negative judgements about other people, their appearance, behaviour, attitudes, etc ... I could stop comparing as soon as I realise what I'm doing, allowing myself and others to simply be as they are.

If I find myself comparing myself – favourably or unfavourably – with someone else ... I could stop comparing as soon as I realise what I'm doing, allowing myself and others to simply be as they are.

A story: Retribution

'Master,' said the young novice, 'many years previous, my brother was killed by a malicious and malevolent robber who murdered him for the trifling amount of money he had in his possession. Try as I might, I am unable to forgive this malevolent miscreant and I would see that he receives in-kind retribution for the pain he has caused my family and me. In truth, many have been the nights when I have dreamed of plunging a dagger into the heart of this monster.'

'My son,' said the master, 'do your thoughts of harming this man, harm him in any way?'

'No master they do not, but they most certainly disturb my sleep with images of murderous retribution.'

'So your thoughts do no harm to anyone but yourself. Is this so my son?'

'Yes, master, I understand that this is so.'

'If you were to act out these thoughts and seek retribution by killing this man, would this lessen in any way the love you have for your brother? Would your brother's heavenly love for you be augmented in any way by your seeking such retribution?'

'No master, my love for my brother is total and nothing on heaven or earth can change it.'

'Good,' said the master, 'then let your thoughts rest securely in the arms of this love you have for him. Let your thoughts spring forth from this love. If you do this, then all of your actions will be as one, and in communion with God Almighty.'

'I say to you sincerely that all that springs from thoughts of malice and revenge will only result in pain and sorrow. All that blossoms from love for yourself and others as yourself will be according to the divine will of God.'

... and we return to the (other side) of the pond:

An imposing figure stood erect, staring out through the large arched windows of his beautifully ornate room, into the garden beyond. This large duck was draped in a cloak of black, with a high neck lined with ermine, to keep away the winter chill.

There was a rapid knock on the double doors leading into this imposing duck's chamber.

'Enter,' was the simple yet assertive command.

Without turning around, the duck said to the vassal who had

entered the room, 'Have you brought me what I seek?'

'Yes master, I have,' said the now trembling vassal, as he placed the package with a thud on his master's desk

'Good, you have done well. And did you do as I commanded and ensure that the security tapes were properly erased?'

'Yes master, this was also completed.'

'Excellent, I am pleased with your work and you are to be rewarded. I have prepared a drink for you in anticipation of your good work.' Then, pointing to a tumbler of liquid positioned on the edge of the desk, he continued, 'Drink and I will then ensure that your efforts are properly rewarded.'

The vassal took a large draft of the elixir that his master had offered. Of a sudden he began to feel his blood pressure rise and his head begin to swoon, then his vision began to blur. Within moments the vassal duck collapsed on the floor, dead. The master duck then casually walked over to his desk and pressed a button to engage the microphone connected to his assistants' outside the room.

'Come and collect the body and dispose of it in the river as I have instructed you,' was the strident command. At which the duck resumed his position of gazing fixedly outside his window, oblivious to the noise of his assistants removing the body of the dead vassal from the room.

Meanwhile ...

On the other side of the pond, there was considerable activity both inside and outside the community's library. Inside, the police were conducting forensic examinations of all of the fixtures and features within the room that had previously housed the sacred text. They were also taking DNA swabs from all of the library personnel and visitors of that day. Quite a monumental task it was, and one that, after considerable time and effort, had presented very little in the way of compelling evidence or leads as to the whereabouts of the book. The only skerrick of evidence that looked remotely like being helpful was a small feather that was found next to the stand on which the book had been stationed. But that was all. It was apparent that the perpetrators of the crime had been most thorough and careful in planning and executing the theft.

Outside of the library was a maelstrom of press vans, reporters and journalists, all seeking a scoop of information that would satisfy the ravenous deadlines of their respective news outlets. Indeed, when Monique ventured out into the foyer of the library, she was set upon by a multitude of eager reporters bombarding her with questions and statements of intent. Now, although she was feeling relatively composed, Monique could sense her stomach tighten into a ball of anguish, and her facial expression was one of steely determination. This is an excerpt of what she had to say to the waiting media:

> Ladies and Gentlemen, as you are all aware, our sacred book, *The Book of Mysteries,* has been stolen from our library. This book, as you know, was the founding inspiration that lead to the construction of our community's world-renowned library. It was written by my great grandfather, Alfred, and was delivered as a treasure to our community by none other than my father, Benjamin, whom many of you knew, loved and respected.
>
> The theft of this sacred tome is considered an affront to the very fabric of our community and society. The words and wisdom in this sacred text represent wisdom that has been passed down through the generations of our duck culture and history. The teachings identify opportunities for the future generations of our children and grandchildren to learn, prosper and evolve, not only as a culture - but as a species. The theft of the book represents a moral outrage by reprehensible individuals and we promise to leave no stone unturned in retrieving this sacred document.

A reward of $100,000 is hereby posted for information leading to the arrest of the perpetrators and return of *The Book of Mysteries* to its rightful place here in the library. I will have more to say about the progress of the investigations as times go forward.

Thank you for your attention.

Realisation rather than Righteousness:

It is with awe that I regard the numerous events and experiences in my life. Now, as I get older, it is far simpler than it was when I was younger to appreciate the majestic nature of the journey that I have undertaken in pursuit of my life's evolution. Yes, far simpler now, than it was in days of my youth. I believe the principle cause for this change in perspective is that I am beginning to relish life's experiences, rather than just evaluate them.

Let me explain.

The human mind has a particularly nasty habit of evaluating everything we do and feel. We regard things as 'agreeable or disagreeable'. Some experiences bring us happiness, some suffering. Other experiences are perceived as pleasant, others painful. These 'conceptions' are polarities based primarily on what we perceive from within our personal limited frames of reference; they include our wants and desires and inherent motivations.

According to Sanchez & Vieira (2007):

> *The ego views our identity as completely separate and has an addictive habit of seeing things from this extremely narrow, one-pointed fixed perspective. The "I" is seen as separate from everyone, everything and anything, and every circumstance. It evaluates from the perspective that is separate: I like, I don't like, I see, I feel. The "I" sees itself as apart from all that it perceives.*

Life is a wonderful journey. Yet, to enhance the fullest realisation of our experiences, we can be better served by acknowledging the limits of our knowledge and understanding. Better this than revelling in the mistaken belief that our own understanding is complete. That our current level of enlightenment has taken us to the final stage of intelligent evolution.

For example, we can acknowledge that there are many things about life/God/the universe that we do not (as yet) understand. We can conclude that we are continually in a state of striving to attain better knowledge and understanding. We could, most certainly, recognise that many of the things we do in our lives are not working, i.e. they are not producing the results that we genuinely seek. Within such a context, we could also be willing to accept new understanding and revelations as they appear.

Righteousness, on the other hand, is the antithesis of such statements for the fulfilment of our evolution. It dulls our senses to the richness of life's ever evolving experiences. It deems that all is known about a particular topic of consideration and, most certainly, accepts that the guardians of this knowledge and understanding are 'bastions of that which is right' and that separates them from other 'mere mortals' like us. So much so, that to gain personal understanding of such doctrines, of necessity, we become beholden to the purveyors of this supposedly superior wisdom and knowledge.

A story: Misery

The young novice was curled up in a foetal position on the floor of her dormitory. It was evident that she was enduring feelings of great abjectness and desolation. Her tears of lament were many and the power of her sobbing was making her body suffer cramps of pain and anguish.

The mistress of the abbey chanced by the dormitory at this time and happened to espy the young novice in her suffering.

'Young novice, what ails you so?' was the compassionate

question from the mistress of the abbey.

'Mother,' said the novice through laboured breaths, 'my life is such a misery. I do not know why I go on. I have a mind to end it all right here and now and face the consequences of the life ever after.'

The mistress was sorely taken by the anguish of her novice and her heart was immediately open to the suffering of her young charge.

'My daughter, I feel your anguish as if it were my own and most truly have I also been in a similar situation to your own, not many years ago.'

'You have?' said the young novice in amazement. 'But you are the mistress of the abbey and the guiding spirit for us all. How is it that you could endure such pain and suffering and wish to end your days on this earth?'

'I, like you young novice, have depths of feelings that are not limited by what others tell us we should think or feel. What you feel is real for you and you must acknowledge it to be so. But I say to you in truth that that which ails you today can best be remedied through the love and compassion you will find in yourself as the truly bright star and divine child of the universe - that you are.

You should never, ever doubt that you are a blessed child of God the Almighty. Whether you are a mistress or a novice, you are no lesser or greater in the eyes of God, who truly loves you beyond measure.'

'But mistress, others in this abbey have called me vile names and they denigrate my heritage because of the colour of my skin and the poverty of my upbringing.'

'These things, young novice, I will most certainly address so that I may enlighten the understanding of others within the abbey. But first we must see to your wellbeing through lessons in finding self-worth and self-love. These will form the basis of your future growth and understanding of life's experiences. You will come to my chamber for one hour every day forthwith for these lessons and instructions. In the meantime, I will see to the enlightenment of others within the abbey through the opportunity for hard work and compassion for all sentient beings.'

... and we return to the pond:

For Monique, the weeks since the theft of the famed manuscript had surely tested her levels of patience and composure. To be sure, she was generally not one to hold back when the need for action dominated. Her attendance on the police department to conduct their investigations was a necessity required by the laws of the community, but the speed at which these investigations occurred tested the resolve of the former investigative journalist.

Actually, Monique felt completely conflicted between her desire to undertake her own covert investigations and her need to remain in control of the library's continual day-to-day operations, under the auspices of its governing constitution.

It was some two weeks post the event that Monique resolved to call upon her new friend and mentor, Gabriel, not just to seek his counsel, but to discuss the dilemma that she was now facing.

She explained the complexity of her dilemma to her friend who sat passive, but engaged, as Monique relayed her thoughts and feelings.

Finally, Gabriel gave expression to his innermost thoughts by asking a direct question.

'Monique, what is your heart's desire in this matter?'

'I would see *The Book of Mysteries* returned to its rightful place in the library. I want the book and its contents to be a legacy for all future generations of ducks. This, I believe, is the ultimate gift that the book bestows upon our culture and our heritage.'

'Very well!' exclaimed Gabriel. 'Then your thoughts are best served by actions that will lead to your direct involvement in the book's ultimate recovery, are they not?'

'Yes, they certainly are,' Monique responded and at the same time a quaint smile lit her face. It was a smile that said, "I know exactly what to do". But before she could rush off to commence the tasks that would begin what was most certainly to be a momentous life experience, Gabriel, added a tremulous note of caution.

'My friend, before you go traipsing off on this perilous endeavour, I fear that your perspective is limited in its scope.'

'What do you mean, 'limited in its scope'? I've got all of my previous life experience as an investigative journalist, and the considerable clout of the library's organisational status and renown at my disposal.'

'Yes, that is correct, but your vision is to recover the book for the cultural and heritage value it has for our community, and you fail to take into consideration that *The Book of Mysteries* is a religious symbol, not just a cultural one. As such, you need to be very careful, for the paths that you will cross are destined to be very powerful, as well as ultimately self-righteous.'

Monique pondered the words of her mentor and said, 'I will be careful'. But in truth her thoughts were now firmly focussed upon the tasks that lay before her in her quest. So immediately afterwards she took one month's extended leave of absence from the library. Her decision came as quite a shock to the library's executives and staff, not to mention the assembled media. She told no one of her plans to investigate the book's disappearance.

Chapter 4

The Pursuit of Justice is Replete with Pitfalls of Morality.

... we return to the ducks

The door of her apartment swung open as Monique attempted to put the key in the lock. Her pulse immediately started to race and small beads of sweat appeared on her brow. She knew this was not normal, as she was habitually careful about the security of her property. All was in darkness as she peered into the hallway, but the usual serenity of her abode was now replaced by a tension that was tangible, though as yet unidentifiable.

'Is anybody there?' she cried into the darkness, the tension in her throat rising.

Not really expecting an answer, she fumbled around for the light switch and what she saw made her stomach reach. So much so, that she almost gagged on the bile that had risen in her throat.

Her living room was a total shambles. Furniture was upturned and smashed. All of her precious pictures and pottery were in strips and shards all over the floor. Her lounge had been ripped and all of its contents strewn about the room. It was a scene of chaos and mayhem. But when she moved to her bedroom, what she saw was even worse. Her bedroom wall was covered in what looked like excrement, and hanging from her bedroom mirror was the carcass of a gutted, dead cat, whose blood had run in rivulets down the glass. Underneath this ghastly scene, the message was scrawled, in blood:

"If you try to find the book, this will be your fate!"

Monique, once again felt nausea reaching up into her throat and it took all of her willpower to stop herself from disgorging the remnants of her last meal. She needed fresh air and immediately ran through the front door, to gasp in some cool air. That tempered her psyche, before she once again found the courage to re-confront the carnage that had once been her home. After a few moments she found that her analytical mind kicked back into gear, and she made the first essential call to the police department to report the offence. Five minutes later, the police were on her doorstep.

The remainder of the evening was a maelstrom of investigations, fingerprinting, DNA swabs, and repetitious answers to repetitive questions from a variety of police officials. She was totally exhausted after the evening's ordeal and in the end was happy to collapse, completely spent, on the bed of the hotel room she had booked after the police left. Despite her exhaustion, sleep did not come as an amicable companion that evening. Her mind was full of anxiety, turmoil, and catastrophe.

'Who in God's name would do such a thing? Why has this happened to me? How am I ever going to cope?'

These were but a few of the many questions that troubled her that evening.

In the morning, when she awoke, it was as if she had never even slept and her first glance in the mirror showed an unfamiliar face that looked as if it had been hit by a freight train. Despite this trauma, however, her stoic determination kicked in and compelled her to go downstairs to the restaurant and break her fast. This, it should be said, made her feel more like a functional member of the species of ducks. Part of the trouble, she realised, was that the events had occurred so suddenly, without any warning. That made them all that much harder to fathom. Indeed, she felt as if her world had collapsed around her and her sense of stability was now being dragged through the mire. Truth be known, seeing all of her possessions in ruin and her home violated was a pain like the death of someone really close.

A Story: Sharks go after the wounded swimmer

The young novice was not long into his tenure at the abbey and the stress of being away from his family caused him to feel a great sense of longing and, at times, abject loneliness. Many were the nights when he would cry himself to sleep. His pillow grew wet with tears of longing for his mother and father, and each night became a struggle to find any sense of peace and security in his heart.

While the sound of his tears was muffled by the soft eider of his pillow, others within the abbey's dormitory heard his lament, but were not at all pre-disposed to offer assistance or sympathy. In fact, a number of the other novices berated and chided the young boy as a 'sissy' and a 'mummy's boy'. They even went so far as to intimidate the young lad with cruel and malicious pranks that caused him to embarrass himself in front of the other boys. All of this just added to the young man's discomfiture.

One day, as the young novice was walking around the courtyard, he was set upon by three other novices who took pleasure in intimidating him.

'Well, if it isn't the little mummy's boy all on his own,' said the first of the antagonists. 'Let me see some of those tears,' he sneered, as he proceeded to push the young novice to the ground and rub the heel of his foot into the chest of the now terrified boy.

'Go away and leave me alone,' was the plaintive cry, but all to no avail, as the other two intimidators took courage from the first to rain a similar level of physical abuse on the distressed young man.

'You there! Stand exactly where you are and do not move,' came an assertive command from the abbey's martial arts master, as he made his way around the corner of the courtyard.

'Take your foot off that novice immediately and let him stand up,' was the next curt command, but be warned. 'If you even think about running away I will not be answerable for the consequences, and you will be in more trouble than you already are.'

As the young novice rose from the ground and made a cursory effort to wipe the dust, grime, and tears from his face, the master gave him a stern but compassionate gaze that reassured him that everything would be all right.

'You three,' he commanded, pointing to the three antagonists, 'I am going to offer you an opportunity, and to you,' now pointing to the young novice, 'I am also going to offer an opportunity.'

'The opportunity I am going to offer each of you three boys is this: if you three combined can best me in a contest, I'll ensure that you don't suffer any further consequences in this matter. In other words, you'll get off scot-free. I'll add further to your advantage by participating in the contest with only my left arm. I will not use my right arm even though I prefer it. However, if you choose not to engage in this contest, perhaps because you are too scared or unwilling to fight an equal, you will be punished with three months of kitchen duty, as well as extra time spent in solitary meditation learning the lessons of humility, empathy and understanding for others. Do you accept these conditions?'

The three boys looked at one another and it was plain to see that all three were totally in fear of the master's renowned prowess. But they knew they had little choice, other than combat, because the alternative, punishment, was harsh indeed.

'We choose to fight,' said the leader of the three, and they began to circle the martial arts master.

At the same time, the master tied his preferred hand to his waist with his sash so that it would be inoperable throughout the course of the contest. The first of the three boys aimed a blow at the master's head, but it was an easy matter for the master to dodge the blow and, at the same time, cause the boy to over balance and land face first in the dust of the courtyard. The second and third boy, seeing their companion's plight, attacked in unison, only to find that their respective heads came knocking together with a sickening sound. The master also ensured that they both ended up with their noses firmly connected to the cobblestones.

'Stand up, all of you,' was the assertive command from the master and he looked firmly into the eyes of each of the three boys.

'Henceforth, you each have a choice to make! You can continue to bully and intimidate others, or, you may choose to attain your higher potential, and learn the skills of empathy, understanding, and compassion for all sentient beings, human and animal. But be warned! If you choose the former, you can be assured that you will endure great pain, anguish and punishment, in both this life and the next, for, in life, what you do to others, you ultimately do to yourself. The divine law of the universe is, "As you sow, so shall you reap". Should you choose the latter, you will be blessed with the greatest opportunity to realise your highest worth in this lifetime. What do you choose?'

The three boys hung their heads in shame and deference to the master's great martial arts prowess and wisdom, and asserted that they would seek only the highest good for themselves and others.

'Good! That is wise,' said the master. 'But you, young novice, you must also know that this harsh experience affords you a great opportunity. You may now decree any punishment you deem fitting for the crime these three miscreants have carried out on you. But be warned, whatever you decree, I shall ensure that it is carried out to the letter.'

At this, you could see the anguished expressions of the three antagonists and the look of fear that entered their eyes. You could also see the turmoil on the face of the young novice, who had been given such an opportunity for revenge against his assailants.

After many moments of thought, the young novice said, 'Master I choose, as punishment for these three, that they must join together with me in training and tutelage under your guidance to master all of the martial arts ... until such time as we have all attained the highest proficiency. However, should any of us fail or revert to our previous ways, we are each to be excommunicated from your tutelage and from the abbey.

'Young novice,' said the master, 'your choice is accepted, for it represents a judgement without malice and offers you all a grand opportunity to realise your highest ambitions, both individually and collectively.'

... and so it was the three became the four, and each of the young boys grew into great achievement and grand friendship.

Challenging Perspective:

Managing stress and stressful situations is an elemental part of the human experience. Bullying in childhood is but one such example. All of us experience varying degrees of stress each day of our lives. This stress can be debilitating (distress) or it can be exhilarating (eustress). How we look at it has much to do with how we react to it.

According to Herman (1992),

> Traumatic events call into question basic human relationships. They breach the attachments of family, friendship, love, and community. They shatter the construction of the self that is formed and sustained in relation to others. They undermine the belief systems that give meaning to human experience. They violate the victim's faith in a natural or divine order and cast the victim into a stage of existential crisis.

Yet, according to Truman (1991),

> People talk about being under a great deal of stress, or something that is stressful to them. Stress is blamed for problems and suffering by everyone. But, how could one identify your stress or my stress? What is stress to one person

may not be stressful to another. In other words, what a STRESSOR is to you may not be a STRESSOR to me.

What these quotations outline is the nature of 'how we think' about stressful situations and the effects that it can cause. One way to realign the consequences of stressful situations is to change the way we think about them, to alter our perspective of the situation or person that causes us to feel stress. In other words we make a *paradigm shift* in how we think about it.

Here are some examples:

Old Thinking	*New Thinking*
"It's too hard, I can't do it."	"I *can* deal with this situation."
"There's nothing that I can do."	"What can I do about it right now."
"There's not enough time."	"I'll make time for what's important."
"Not again, I can never cope with these situations."	"I've handled these situations before, I *can* do it again."

... back to the pond:

As she sat and mused over her morning breakfast, Monique couldn't help but feel entirely violated. She reasoned that it was only her personal possessions and property that were defiled and destroyed. These could all be replaced in time. Yet within her being, it was as if she had somehow been stripped of her sense of self-respect, and a personal indignity had been cast upon her.

She wondered what sort of depraved, immoral mind would even design, let alone act upon, urges to conduct such an affront to another person's property. Not to mention the foul act to the cat and the malicious message that the perpetrator had left as a legacy. Surely, she mused, people who commit such foul deeds must be totally evil and lack any kind of moral compass.

All of a sudden, in the midst of these musings, she felt a great urge for revenge.

'I'll find these people if it is the last thing I do,' she hissed, 'and when that happens, I'll do my utmost to ensure that they receive the full force of the law.'

At least, she argued, this would save others from having to endure the same pain as had been inflicted on her by this foul individual.

Then, as soon as these vengeful thoughts filled her consciousness, she began to feel tremors of fear. Mostly, she remembered the warning of the blood-soaked message on the mirror.

'My God, this really is terrifying,' she said to herself, 'someone is very determined to ensure that *The Book of Mysteries* is never found. That they are willing to go to lengths such as this is quite extraordinary.'

Of a sudden, her body started to shake uncontrollably and she had to place her hands under her torso so that nobody would see the abject terror she now felt. The thought that somebody really was prepared to kill her, cast a tremulous chill down the back of her spine and caused her stomach to twist into knots of anguish.

'Maybe I should just leave it to the police to sort out this mess,' she thought. 'At least then I'll be safe and they won't come after me.'

With so much confusion in her mind and with all the stress coursing through her veins, she closed her eyes for a moment, and then pictured speaking to her mother and father in the quiet recesses of her heart.

'Mum and Dad,' she said quietly, 'I really am in trouble now and I need your counsel. What am I supposed to do?'

It was then that she sensed, rather than heard, the answer to her question. It was her mother's serene presence that she sensed most of all.

'The answers to your problems do not come from outside. The answer to all of life's problems lies within you. Take responsibility for your own problems and your misguided efforts. Do not blame others. Merely follow the pathway of your own TRUTH.'

The shrill ring of her mobile phone interrupted her musings and brought her back to the present moment. It was the reporter from the *Pond Post*. Indeed, it never ceased to amaze her how assiduous some of these reporters were in sniffing out the latest news story – all in the community's best interest they would point out.

Monique managed to delay meeting the reporter until later that morning. After such time, she hoped to get her thoughts in order and plan her next course of action in this affair. She felt it was getting way too big for her to handle on her own.

A story: The Mistress's anguish

The mistress of the abbey was sorely vexed this very evening. She had just received an express epistle from none other than Her Divine Mistress the leader of her order and divine orator of the spoken word of her religion. The letter read:

> My dearest Mary,
> I regret to inform you that, by divine decree, your abbey is to be closed no later than thirty days from the date of this letter.
>
> The past few years have seen a decline in the number of parishioners and devotees at your abbey, and the holy order no longer believes that your abbey can contribute a financially viable service for the benefit of the local community. Your divine work at the abbey over many years has been without peer, yet each abbey must continue to demonstrate a capacity for growth and expansion irrespective of previous success.
>
> As always, I remain your friend and devotee to the word of God the Almighty.
>
> Yours

Mary Benedict
Mother Superior

Many were the tears that flowed in the privacy of the mistress's chamber that day. Indeed, her attending novices became greatly concerned at the absence of their mistress from her duties. Normally, she applied herself to them so diligently. One young novice attempted to enter, knocking many times on the door of her chamber, all to no avail. Finally, the mistress bade enter the young novice who sought her attention.

'Mistress, we have been sorely concerned for you – are you alright?' was the plaintive query from the young novice.

'Yes, my child, I am alright, but sometimes the weight of the office of mistress can be as onerous as the weight of the world.'

'But mistress, what could be so bad that it causes you such evident and unusual stress. I have never before seen you with such a heavy spirit?'

'My child, it is true that my heart is deeply troubled, but it is a matter about which I cannot as yet speak with you. First I must reconcile my actions with the duties I have to perform, and these are much in conflict with the feelings in my heart.'

'Mistress,' said the young novice, 'might I be permitted to tell you a short story?'

'Yes, indeed you may, my child.'

'When I was a young girl, my mother said that I had to go away and live with my father. She had been separated from him for some years. I felt lonely, devastated and adrift. I felt as if my mother no longer loved or cared for me and at first, I called her vile names and abused her for being a bad mother.

... and you know, I moved in with my father, who through his grace and kindness allowed me to follow my vocation to become a novice of this abbey. What I now know is that without the pain of separation from my mother all of those years ago, I would not be here with you today in God's holy order, and that is a greater gift than any other.'

'Thank you, my child. For one so young your wisdom is most profound, and now I know what I must do. Furthermore, I will fulfil these tasks with a heart filled with peace, purpose and determination, not anguish, malice or negativity. The blessings of the spirit be upon you my child.'

Passion and Purpose is the Positive:

I wrote in *The Music of the Soul,* (2011),

> Passion releases energy. The challenges that we face in pursuit of our goals can be overcome through the perseverance inherent in the energy of our passion. It is not a domination, nor an attempt to defeat or vanquish, but a passion to realise our vision and fulfil our dreams.

If we have such a passion and are committed to fulfilling our vision or purpose, our feelings will then be inherently positive, filled with the promise of possibility. By their very nature, these positive feelings will displace and diffuse any self-defeating feelings of negativity or stress.

It is as Trumann (1991) states

> When you recognize your feelings of discomfort, uneasiness, irritation or whatever the stressful feeling may be, you are identifying your negative feelings and owning them (admitting they are actually there). At this point, you are no longer in denial and half the challenge is over.

... and back to the pond:

The doors of the large chamber flew open and the undeniable presence of the master filled the room with the energy of radiated power and authority. He was dressed in a cloak of black that cascaded from neck to toe, and was lined in immaculate red satin that shimmered when the reflected light caught its corners. All of the other members of the council were duly in attendance at the meeting, and were seated around the large and ornate boardroom table, in solemn attendance upon their master and patriarch.

'The meeting of the Council of the Brotherhood of Ecumenical Light is now in progress,' boomed the voice of the master as he took control of the proceedings.

First on the order of business was the report on the continued induction of members into the Brotherhood, while the second item was an overview of the current position of the order's finances. Both were duly presented to the satisfaction of the master, and the acquiescence of the other assembled members. Finally, after all of the regular items of business had been discussed and addressed, the master motioned for silence, in view of the very important announcement that he was about to make.

'As you all know, over these past many months, I have been sorely troubled by the continued dissemination of sacrilegious and profane works and writings amongst the brethren of our community. I have been in solemn communication with the Almighty about these matters. I now decree that these writings are an outrage against the very name of God and His divine works and words. They have fostered a delusion that is evil, an outrage against the very name of our order that works against our divine mission. It has to be stopped for it is an offence against God Almighty.

I declare to you today that I have taken steps to ensure that this evil can no longer exist. By my order, the divine word of God will continue to be spread in its truth and sacred purpose through His messengers of the Holy Order of the Brotherhood of Ecumenical Light. We of your divine holy order, are now in possession of the so-called, *Book of Mysteries,* which was once viewed as an icon and centrepiece of our community's library.

However, in making this declaration, I also give you warning. Should any word of these matters be heard outside of the walls of this sacred room, I will ensure that the purveyors of such malicious gossip will taste the vileness of their words in the blood on their tongues. They will be excommunicated from our holy order, and cast out from Heaven into eternal hellfire, in the name of God the Almighty. Does each of you swear before God that your tongues are forever silenced on this matter?'

As the master said these words, he cast his gaze into the eyes of each individual member. It was as if he was peering into their very souls. There was nowhere to hide from his piercing and compelling intrusion into the psyche.

'We do,' came the communal assent from the members.

But there was one who did not so swear! One of the assembly had managed to swallow his fear and trembling, enough to pronounce those two simple words. But his soul remained conflicted. He was inclined to suspect that evil events had occurred and his conscience was in turmoil, despite his ever-present fear and trepidation for what might befall him if the master were to learn of his doubts.

... Meanwhile:

It was well past the aperitif hour when Monique returned to her hotel room after meeting with the reporter from the *Pond Post*. The interview itself had gone well. While she gave an outline of the basic facts of the robbery at her home, Monique made no mention of the dead cat or the message written in blood. She also thought better than to say anything about her intention to pursue her own investigations into the disappearance of *The Book of Mysteries*.

'Better to be safe than sorry' she thought, and more than that, she still felt an undeniable tinge of fear and concern for her wellbeing should her intentions be made public.

Meanwhile, on the other side of the pond, the police were

recovering a body of a dead duck from under the trees and shrubs that covered the bend just beyond the edges of the pond. It appeared that the body of the deceased duck had washed up with the ebb of the waterfall that feeds the pond with its clear, refreshing flow of water. It was particularly beneficial in the warmer summer months of the year, but not so now.

An initial examination suggested that the duck had been deceased for some seven to eight days, but decay and rigor mortis had already begun to make identification of the body a task that would require time and concerted effort. What was evident, however, was that someone had gone to considerable lengths to hinder the proper identification of the body. All external extremities that would normally aid the identification process had been severed from the corpse. This was undoubtedly a murder of the most heinous kind.

Monique, on the other hand, completely oblivious of the occurrence on the other side of the pond, had managed to make a phone call to her primary source and contact within the local police department. Louise had been a friend of Monique's since their school days and had chosen to make a career in the police force, while Monique had preferred to become an investigative journalist. Both had remained friends over the years and on the odd occasion had helped one another out with information, a lead or a tip-off as and when required.

'Louise, how are you doing?' asked Monique.

'Hey Monique, I heard that you got into a bit of trouble with a robbery at your house. Are you okay?'

'Yeah, okay now. I was a bit shook up at first, but I'm alright now.'

'Um ... Monique, did you hear about the body they found at the other side of the pond last night? It seems that it's a murder investigation, and that whoever did the crime did a good job of concealing their tracks. The body was mutilated almost beyond description.'

'God, how awful! There sure are some strange things happening around our pond of late. First the theft of *The Book of Mysteries,* then my house gets trashed, I get threatened, and now someone is found murdered.'

'Monique, I want you to take real good care of yourself, do you understand? Whoever committed these crimes has some seriously bad intent and I don't want anything to happen to you. Do you hear me?'

'Yes Louise, I hear you loud and clear. Don't worry. I'll be careful. By the way, did anything ever turn up with the DNA report on that feather? You know – the one they found in the room next to the stand where the book was kept.'

'No, nothing yet, but as soon as anything breaks I'll let you know. We're still searching our database but haven't turned up anything yet.'

'Great, thanks Louise, I'll talk to you soon. Bye.'

Chapter 5

Be Ready, Willing and Able

A Story: The Master's address ...

The master was addressing his congregation of novices and monks, gathered to hear him proclaim the dawn of the New Year and give his annual 'state of the nation' address. It was customary at the abbey that the address should be presented to all initiates of the order. Thus might they be given direction and fortitude to serve to the best of their abilities in the forthcoming year.

When the abbot entered the sacred hall, those assembled rose to their feet as one and bowed deeply before the master, acknowledging his presence and his wisdom. The master, in turn, most humbly acknowledged the respect of the assembled monks and initiates by placing his hands in the position of prayer and pronouncing a divine blessing upon the members of the order. When the master spoke, all listened in attentive awe of his reverence. For, it was he who had guided the abbey and its novices through many turbulent years of war and pestilence in the outside world.

The master said:

> 'Behold, I am a servant of God most Holy. Yet I am only a man. Like you, I have limitations, foibles and inconsistencies. I am not perfect, nor do I seek perfection in this life. However I, like each of you, have a divine purpose in this lifetime as long as my spirit inhabits my body. This divine purpose is, for me, an irresistible force that is totally compelling and divinely inspired. This divine purpose is my intimate connection to my true being, my true self.
>
> As I stand before you today, I declare that you need only three undeniable qualities to remain in accord with the

Universe that gave you the gift of life everlasting.

The first and foremost is *"readiness"*.

You must be ready to accept that much of what you are currently doing in your life is not working. You must be ready to accept that there are aspects of God and the wider Universe that you do not understand. You must be ready to acknowledge that your current state of existence is unacceptable and that you must be open to explore new ideas of functionality, adaptability and sustainability. You must be ready to dispense with old ideas, doctrines and paradigms that no longer serve you well. Additionally, you must be ready to acknowledge the divinity in all of man's beliefs, creeds and cultures. It is not enough to follow just your own divine doctrines to the exclusion of others.

The second quality is *"willingness"*.

As a child of God, you can demonstrate your willingness to embrace your divine purpose through commitment and courage. Life will present obstacles. Your challenges will be as great as you perceive them to be. Yet, I say to you, that all of these will be overcome. No wall will be too high for those of you who have the courage to persist in the face of adversity. In the presence of divine purpose, all walls will be cast asunder.

Your willingness must also reside in your ability to cast aside that which does not serve you well. Do not become lost in servitude to the impermanent or unreliable. Fame, wealth and power are all illusions. They reek of impermanence and cast their spell upon the weak and feeble minds of those who seek solace in their fleeting embrace. But you should be more concerned with service to others, to the brotherhood of all men of peace and goodwill. Yet, should conflict ensue in pursuit of your purpose, I say to you, 'Gird your loins in courage and fortitude, so that you may fulfil your divinely inspired destiny.'

The last quality is *"ability"*.

You must have the ability to change the way you think. For, if you can change the way you think, then you can change your experience of the world around you. In fact, much of what you think is based on past experience and habitudes. If you can but open your mind to new or enhanced perspectives, then your experience of life will be much enriched. All new experiences come with the blessings of the divine. Ask yourself, 'Does this thought serve me well?' or 'How can I better perceive this experience or situation?' and you will begin the journey of enlightenment and freedom away from the bondage of a limited perspective.

In truth, I say to you all, be ready, willing and able in all aspects of your life. Then the blessings of the universe will be with you in abundance for all days of your life.'

... and we return to the pond:

Once absent from her normal abode, and away from the daily tribulations of her job as General Manager of the Library, Monique discovered that she had more time to reflect on her current predicament. That is, she found she had more time to think creatively about her circumstances. This meant that instead of merely reacting to the problems and obstacles that she was confronted with, she was better able to allow her creative mind to seek solutions from the limitless resources of her sub-conscious.

One particular morning, she felt an urge to take a walk under the bridge, just near where the murdered body had been discovered. God knows why she went for a walk this way because it was well away from her usual routine even to come within a kilometre of this area. Yet, here she was, strolling for some unknown reason and looking for goodness knows what. Then, all of a sudden, her gaze briefly caught a reflection of something partially concealed by reeds and rocks. Her curiosity piqued, she went to investigate. What she saw made her pulse quicken and her heart skip a beat. It was a knife and it was plain to see that there was dried, coagulated blood still on the hilt and the blade.

Slowly, with the greatest caution, she removed a handkerchief from her cloak and placed the knife into her carry bag. Furtively, she looked around to see if anyone was in the vicinity, or had seen her place the knife into her bag.

'What have I done?' she thought to herself. 'Surely this is a matter for the police.' But then again she knew that possession of the knife would lead to her becoming the subject of accusations that she had previously not thought about.

She made a phone call …

'Louise, it's Monique. We need to talk, and quick.'

'Why? What's the matter? What's happened? Are you okay?'

'Yes, but we need to meet, and it needs to happen in private. I'll meet you at the café by the southern bend in the pond in half an hour. Don't tell anyone that you are meeting me and make sure you come alone.'

'Monique you are scaring me, but I'll be there in thirty minutes.'

Creativity – the essence:

Are you ready to be creative? Do you believe that you can be? Are you willing to give it a go?

If you answered 'yes' to each of these questions, then okay, let me give you the essential secrets to being creative. But this is not a lesson in creative writing, sculpting or painting. Nor is it an essay on 'how to do' any of these wonderful things. Rather, it is about making room in your life, (that is, finding the space and time) for creativity to happen.

Do you remember the old saying, "Let me sleep on it"? Have you ever gone to bed with a question or problem on your mind, only to wake up in the morning (or middle of the night) with the solution in the forefront of your mind? So much so that you have to immediately find a notebook to write down the solution. Often, you wonder why you were so perplexed about the problem in the first place ... the answer now seems so obvious.

What has happened? Well, by going to bed with the problem or issue unresolved in your conscious mind, you have allowed the period of sleep to 'shut-down' the ruminations, analyses and fears of the conscious mind; and you have thus given the sub-conscious mind the opportunity to apply itself creatively to solving the problem. This is a very effective process of creativity, one that I am sure we have all experienced at some time in our lives. But there's a problem if we follow this path to a solution – we have to go to sleep every time we have a problem to solve or a dilemma to unravel. Simple, but impractical most of the time! Yet, we can apply the same principles of creativity in our waking hours. We can allow the same creative forces to work in our conscious mind, and arrive at a solution just the same. To do so we must recognise *three* essential ingredients for creativity, namely:

Create uninterrupted time:

In our effort to allow our creative processes to function to maximum effect, we need to create time without the constant interruption of extraneous activities. That means that the time we allow, whether it is half an hour, one hour or much more, needs to be clear of any distractions – such as, phone calls, the 'pop-up' signal of your email inbox or people knocking on your door demanding your attention. If you allow these interruptions to your creativity, you will have re-engaged the conscious mind on some day-to-day matter, and you will find it much harder to re-engage the creative flow of the sub-conscious mind.

Create uninterrupted space:

As hard as it may be in either our home or workplace environments, it is essential that we create an 'area or recess' in which creativity can occur. This means that you must have an area or room in which you have all the essential resources at your disposal for creativity to occur. If you are a writer, this might be a laptop. If you are a painter, this might be brush, paints and canvas. If you sculpt … well, you get the picture.

While you don't want interruptions to your time, so too you don't want annoying distractions, like searching for resources, the lack of which will hinder the creative process.

Ask creative questions

You need to ask the right questions.

I have previously described this process in *Music of the Soul,* Chong (2011):

> Creative questions generally commence with: 'What', 'How' or 'Where'. These questions are creative of their very nature because, inherently, they challenge the status quo of our current circumstances. *Creative questions* are *drivers* because they challenge us to seek an answer that will improve our current position. These *creative questions* enable us, through clarity of mind, to focus on the present and future, not on the past.

Then, once you have asked the creative question – relax, listen. The answer/inspiration will come. Allow the sub-conscious mind to complete its task.

Remember however, this is NOT a thinking process. It is a LISTENING process.

A Story: The mistress's anguish (continued)

This is the continuing story (from Chapter Four) of the mistress whose dilemma was great after being told that her abbey was to be shut down, by order of her Mother Superior.

After her cathartic experience with her young novice, the

mistress of the abbey summoned her personal assistant into her chamber to take dictation of a letter in response to the epistle from the Mother Superior. She wrote:

Dear Mother Superior,

I am forever the servant of God the Almighty that gives wings to our voices and passion to our hearts. Within our holy order will be found a divine pathway of revelation and redemption for all men and women, irrespective of their race, creed or colour. All who come to our order may do so in the knowledge that they will not be judged for the sins of their past; rather, they will be given the grace of relief from their suffering and release from their guilt and fear.

Many souls have come through the abbey over the years of our service. Whether these souls were here for mere minutes, or for many years – the divine grace they received was without limitation, complete in its abundance.

For myself, I am a mere servant of the order and a vessel for the grace of God here on this earth. Yet, I must say to you — and I am aware of the risk for all that may ensue – that I will not close the abbey as you have directed. The divine purpose of the abbey, in service to the many souls of the community to whom we dedicate our resources, cannot be measured in numbers or dollars. These things are transient, belonging to the world of men – not to the will of divine purpose. If we save but one soul, it is as if we save ourselves.

Therefore, I will continue to follow, to the best of my ability and resources, the divine purpose of the abbey and its initiates, and I am prepared for whatever decree you should now wish to bestow upon me, your humble servant.

Yours in true faith,

Mistress of the Abbey

… and back to the pond:

'Monique, what in God's name is going on?' said Louise as she sat down opposite her friend at the table in the far corner of the café where the light was at its dimmest.

'Take a look at this. I found it just a short distance away from where they found the body of that murdered duck.'

She then showed Louise the knife, still wrapped in its cloth and now concealed in a plastic seal-wrapped package.

'God forbid Monique, why in God's name didn't you leave it where you found it and call the police to come and investigate? Do you realise what you have done by tampering with this evidence? Do you realise that you could incriminate yourself in this ghastly saga?'

At these words, Monique started to feel a tingle of fear cascade down her spine, but nonetheless she persisted with the explanation of her actions.

'Louise, somehow I know that the murder of this duck is linked to the disappearance of The *Book of Mysteries*. I don't know how as yet, but I'm sure there's a connection and I need you to help me find it.'

'Do you realise what you're asking me? You're asking me to pretend that I know nothing about the knife and how it came into my possession. You are, I think, asking me to ignore your involvement in the process and then, no doubt, you will expect me to tell you all about the investigation that results from this new evidence. Do you realise what kind of position you are putting me in here?'

Monique hung her head and closed her eyes for just a few moments. As if she were trying to feel the heaviness of the burden that she had placed upon Louise. Then, after a few moments, she said, 'I wouldn't put you in this position if I was aware of any other pathway to finding out who has taken *The Book of Mysteries* and, by chance, the perpetrator of the murder.'

'Hold on a minute,' said Louise, 'I haven't seen any evidence that links the theft of the book to the murder of that poor duck. This is just some wild speculative assumption that you've come to believe.'

'You're right, but I cannot deny the gut feeling I have that these two events are intimately linked. By the way, have you turned up any evidence on the origin of the feather that was found at the scene of the robbery in the library?'

'Yes, we have, but God knows why I should disclose any of it to you.'

But with a sigh, Louise said, 'The feather belonged to a duck named Horatio. It seems that he was a petty criminal – minor break and enters and possession of drugs, mainly when he was a young teenager. These past couple of years he has been quiet. It seems that he found his religious calling and for the last few years has been linked to that evangelical church group, the Brotherhood of Ecumenical Light, and he has not been any bother to the police since then.'

'I've heard of them. They're the group that are run by that firebrand preacher. Master Vladimir, I think he calls himself doesn't he? I wonder whether he knows anything about this,' said Monique, almost to herself.

'Now don't you go sticking your nose into areas that you know nothing about. Leave it to the police. Let them do their work.'

'Okay, Louise, keep your shirt on, I promise that I'll let the police do what they do best. But have you compared the DNA from the evangelical Horatio, with that of the deceased duck's bodily fluids?' Even though she knew she sounded a trifle condescending, Monique couldn't help it, for in her mind she was formulating her next strategy for retrieving the famous book.

'You leave the Sherlock work to the police. I want you to keep your nose clean from now on. Is that clear?' exclaimed Louise rather piqued at Monique's intrusiveness.

They subsequently left the café with Louise carrying the

parcel wrapped in plastic and muttering something about making up a story about how it came into her possession.

The purpose of a goal is to create an obstacle:

I stated in *The Music of the Soul* (2011), "... that a goal, by its very nature, will create obstacles that must be overcome, challenges that will need to be surmounted."

But, haven't we got enough problems in our lives without creating others? Why should we undertake tasks or activities that merely add to the pile of issues that already confront us?

In *The Book of Testaments* (2009), I invited you to visualise an experience of achieving a goal or a target. "Do you remember how that felt? The euphoria and excitement?" I stated that, "The achievement of this goal assisted with an improved self-image and love of one's self that then indeed enhanced and enriched the lens through which you viewed the world."

Further, a golden rule identified in *The Music of the Soul* (2011), was that, "You never know what you are capable of until you put yourself in a position to find out". But over and above the fact that we never know what we are capable of until we test our limits, we can be *willing* to give things a go – to engage to the best of our ability (not do things by half measures, but really give them total commitment). We are more than capable of approaching everything that we do with the expectation of finding fun and enjoyment, irrespective of the degree of challenge associated with the task, i.e. if we see things as a problem, that's what they will be (perspective creates reality). We are capable of setting small goals, and really nailing them (for the small goals will lead to the larger objective).

... and when all is said and done and you've made it - really enjoy the satisfaction that you did it.

I also described in *The Music of the Soul* (2011), "These *guiding principles* can be engaged despite any feelings of fear, reticence or trepidation. They are more than superficial motivation or hype.

These principles can become a part of our armoury to help us reconceptualise our fears as adventures."

... and we return to the pond

Monique was sitting in the antechamber awaiting her audience with the supreme master of the Brotherhood of Ecumenical Light. Whilst she had arrived early, the meeting was now some thirty minutes overdue. Despite a couple of entreaties to the master's personal assistant, the response was a polite, but cold, 'The master will be with you in a moment.'

All of a sudden, the buzzer sounded on the personal assistant's desk, with an electronically distorted voice commanding, 'The visitor may now enter.'

Monique opened the double doors leading into a vast office that was as overwhelming as it was ostentatious. But what struck her like a hammer blow was the physical presence of the duck who called himself, Master Vladimir. He was huge, probably a span taller than a normal duck. But it was the aura of power that radiated from him that almost made Monique gasp for air. Despite her initial bewilderment, she managed to approach the large ornate desk with confidence and surety. He did not get up or offer any form of formal greeting, but merely got straight down to the inquiry for her visit.

'I understood that you have taken leave of absence from your position at the library, yet you stand before me in this capacity. Why is this so?'

Once again, Monique felt a momentary chill of fear tingle down her spine and she could feel a cold trail of sweat emanate from under her wings, but with a steady voice and direct gaze she said, 'Your grace, I am sure that your Brotherhood has benefited much by the construction and function of our community's library. You are well aware that the library has brought great prosperity to many within our humble pond. Not to mention the significant influx of immigrant ducks who have come to our pond to start their families and ply their trade. Many of these ducks, I am sure, have had need of the spiritual guidance provided by your Brotherhood and have thus found their way to your congregation for spiritual nourishment.'

'Yes, young lady, all of this may be so, but it still does not explain your presence in my office. Our work here at the Brotherhood is inspired by the word of God. Many souls have received the blessings and redemption of the Almighty through our divine inspiration.'

'Your grace, I am sure you are aware that approximately one month ago, we endured a very great loss from the library's treasured accumulation of manuscripts - the theft of *The Book of Mysteries*. I am sure you know that this manuscript was the founding book and inspiration for the construction of the library to which we are all so indebted.'

'Young lady, I would remind you that we in the Brotherhood are indebted to nobody but God, and our faith resides solely in the words of His holy scriptures. Having said that, I can understand your sense of loss for your library's manuscript. But what does that have to do with me?'

'Your grace, with the many resources at your disposal, you may have some information that might lead to the recovery of the manuscript?'

Upon asking this question, Monique saw an almost imperceptible change in the demeanour of Master Vladimir, but it was so quick that it was as if it had never occurred.

'Young lady, in my position as custodian of the holy word of the Brotherhood of Ecumenical Light, I am charged with many different duties, and especially the guidance of many thousands of souls under my stewardship. If I was to ever receive information that would require me to make a declaration to the police to solve a crime, then you can be assured that I would pass this information to the relevant authorities.'

'Your grace, are you telling me that you know nothing about

the disappearance of *The Book of Mysteries*?'

At this question, Master Vladimir stood up and now towered over young Monique.

'Young lady, I am beholden to none other than God the Almighty and I will not have you insinuate that I am in any way in possession of information that can help you. You will leave now and should you ever deign to enter these chambers again, it will be on your knees in supplication to the divine word of God.'

Monique, despite feeling her knees shake, managed to say, 'Thank you for your time your Grace. I will not trouble you further unless it is completely imperative.'

Once outside, Monique could barely take a breath. It was as if the tension had restricted her airways. After a couple of minutes, however, she managed to regain her sensibilities and, with some difficulty on wobbly legs, made her way back to her apartment.

Chapter 6

Every act in life is an act of self-definition

Life, by its very nature, is an accumulation of a multitude of experiences. But more than this, it is a great gift in which we can realise the greatest version of our grandest vision, whilst we still have breath in our bodies.

I conducted a workshop recently and one of the participants, who was on the other side of seventy-five years of age contacted me afterwards and said, 'I've given to others all of my life, and I continue to be disappointed in their response.'

He explained to me that he had always tried to live by some simple, yet profound, principles. He wanted to be a 'good husband', a 'good father' and a 'good provider'. He went on to tell me that he had lost his first wife and son in a motor vehicle accident many years ago and that his second wife had suffered Alzheimer's disease and had recently passed away. Yet, despite all of these life challenges, he explained to me, he always tried to stay positive and to refrain from giving in to despair. I found him to be a beautiful man, full of gentleness and good humour.

In response, and in awe, I said to him that he had accumulated such a wonderful 'cabinetful' of life experiences that they should be passed on to many others so that they, in turn, could learn from his wisdom. Secondly, I stated that wherever we are in life, but particularly when our time on earth begins to approach its end (at a mature age), it is imperative that we gain clarity on what, for us, is our stated 'life purpose'. It is important to know our 'life purpose' at any age, but imperative when we reach the age of maturity.

There can be no greater or compelling force than to know and understand our reason for being - the reason we are here, in this lifetime. I emphasise here that knowing what is, for us, our stated 'life purpose', is more than just a thought process; it is more than a belief. It is a *knowing* based on what we feel and experience, with totality, in our hearts and minds.

In Chong (2011) I said, "We can be purposeful in many areas of our lives, for example:

- Physically – 'I will love and respect my body'
- Mentally – 'I will think only thoughts that serve me well'
- Emotionally – 'I will express my emotions through the prism of love'
- In Relationships – 'I will treasure all of my relationships'
- In Business – 'I will prosper only through the benefit to others'
- With Money – 'I choose abundance and generosity'"

Remember, your life purpose is as individual to you as the fingerprints on your hand. The above are just examples of what may be. Yet, I say to you that, knowledge of your life purpose will be like a guiding light for all your future actions. So much so, that every action then becomes an act of self-definition … of who you really are.

A Story: Why Even Bother to Try?

'Young David, how do you fare today? You look a little dishevelled and upset. Is anything the matter?' said the master to his young novice.

'Master, in truth I feel absolutely terrible. So much so that I wonder why I should go on with this life. All I ever get is trouble, problems and grief.'

'This is not like you, David! Since I have known you, all I've ever observed is a positive and loving outlook. What has turned your thoughts to such trouble and strife?'

'Well master, I've just returned from a visit to my parents' house, only to find that they are getting a divorce. My mother was beside herself with anger. She threw things at me and told me it was 'all my fault'. According to her, if I had been around to support her, this never would have happened. At the same time, my brother has been charged with a heinous crime and looks like spending time in gaol. My God! What else could go wrong? Why do I even bother to try?'

'Precisely, my young novice – why even bother to try?' exclaimed the master.

'But master, what are you saying? Should I just give it all away and jump off a bridge?'

'Not at all, young novice, but understand - there is no 'trying'. You either 'do' or you 'don't do''.

'But master, I do not understand.'

'David,' said the master with much loving kindness, 'life, of its very nature, will present each and every one of us with challenges and obstacles to overcome. Some of these, we will perceive as small, some we will consider as grave and monumental. However, the way you perceive them will certainly be your reality.'

'But master, how am I supposed to deal with all of these problems in my family? What am I supposed to do?'

'Firstly, young David, you do not need to do anything.'

'But surely master, I cannot sit idly by and leave all of these problems to others in my family?'

'Okay then, young man. If these things are important to you, if you treasure these relationships, then you need to be purposeful. Being purposeful in treasuring your relationships will give eloquence to your voice. It will give strength to your arms and courage to your heart. You will have all the resources you need to enable your purpose to be fulfilled.'

'But master, what if they deny my actions and reject my intentions?'

'Yes, young David, this may be so! Yet, if you have given all that you have from your heart, then you have done all that you need to do. The consequences will be for others to bear and not for you to experience.'

... and back to the pond:

It was in a tiny, cramped chamber, one of many within the Brotherhood's expansive grounds and buildings that a duck had prostrated himself on the floor – lying prone before the image of his God on the wall.

'God, what am I to do?' was his lamentable cry.

The anguish of the duck was replete as he smashed his palms into the worn carpet that served as meagre covering to the floor.

'I've tried my best to serve you and now you deliver me this poisoned chalice. What more do you want from me than what I've already given You?'

Tears were not the only expression of his grief, for his forehead was now rubbed red-raw from his prostrations upon the carpet.

'If I but utter a word of the events that I know to have occurred within the Brotherhood, I will surely be carved into little pieces and fed to the dogs. My life will be forfeited, and I will be excommunicated and cast from Heaven. I won't be able to have eternal life. I'll be barred from Paradise. Yet if I stay my hand and speak not a word, my heart will forever be split asunder by guilt and regret for the vile sins that we have committed in Your holy name. What am I to do, please tell me?'

The torment and tears that this duck felt were almost enough to turn his mind to madness and cause his heart to burst from the turmoil.

Some time later Monique received a phone call.

'Meet me under the awnings of the old bridge on the west side at eight o'clock tonight,' said the muffled voice on the phone. 'Come alone. Do not contact the police, and do not bring any recording devices. If you do this, I will give you that which you most seek.'

'Who is this, what is your name?' came the shrill inquiry from Monique. But the phone clicked off – the line went dead.

'My God,' said Monique to herself, 'this is really getting serious. What am I going to do? Chances are that I could be set upon and hurt. Or even worse.' Her body was shaking and her mind was speeding like an unrestrained locomotive.

The time passed very slowly on its way to 8.00 pm that evening and every moment of waiting was like a vice upon her mind in torment. Yet, she was determined to go. She didn't contact anyone, especially the police, but she did take the precaution of leaving a brief note of her actions and whereabouts on her kitchen table in the event of her falling upon foul play.

As she made her way under the eaves of the bridge, the light suddenly disappeared and all she could see were ephemeral shadows of the ramparts and overhangs on the bridge.

'Don't come any closer,' was the abrupt command from a shrill but distinct voice.

'Who are you and what do you want with me?' demanded Monique. 'If you try and harm me, I'll make sure that we'll find out how well you bleed.'

'I mean you no harm,' said the voice, 'but you must understand that if they catch me talking to you, I will be killed – my life will be forfeit to them.'

'Who? Who will kill you? What are you talking about?'

'I know what you seek and I know where it can be found.'

'You mean the book – *The Book of Mysteries*? Do you know where it is?' said Monique in barely restrained excitement.

'The book that you seek is in the possession of the master of the Brotherhood of Ecumenical Light. He has it. He arranged for it to be stolen.'

At this news, Monique let out an involuntary gasp, as if she had been punched in her solar plexus. 'Oh my God! But why? Why did he take it? What good does it do him?'

But there was no answer to these questions, for all she heard was the scampering sound of running footsteps on the cobblestones of the bridge underpass. He was gone. Monique, looked around to see if she could find anything that might help her identify the whistleblower, but alas, all she could find was rubbish blown in by the westerly winds that whistled through its support structure.

With a renewed sense of urgency and a chill at the very centre of her being, she made her way back to the privacy of her apartment.

Meanwhile …

Back at the investigative centre at police headquarters, Louise picked up the phone. It was the lab. They had found a match with the DNA on the knife. With great haste, she made her way down the corridor and into the lift that would take her straight to the laboratory facility.

'What have you found?' asked Louise breathlessly.

'It seems that the deceased was none other than the same Horatio duck that we identified previously. The feather we found at the library has the same DNA as the poor creature we found mutilated by the waterfall.'

Louise didn't even bother to say thank you. She sped back to her office and picked up the phone …

The Value of Values

According to Walsch, N.D. (2002) "Everything you think, say, and do defines you, announces your choice about yourself."

What we think, say and do, i.e. the source of our actions and behaviours, are our values. Values, as defined by The Business Directory (April 2011) are:

> … important and enduring beliefs or ideals shared by members of a culture about what is good or desirable and what is not. Values exert major influence on the behaviour of

> an individual and serve as broad guidelines in all situations.

Similarly, Cole, K. (2005) tells us that:

> Values combine with people's beliefs about themselves, others, and the world around them to guide their actions. Each person's value and belief systems are unique to them, based on their upbringing and life experiences.

Maher Baba (1987) wrote that:

> "True values must govern all matters" and "The life of true values can be spontaneous only when the mind has developed the unbroken habit of choosing the right values".

My understanding of values, and how they influence our lives, is that they are neither right, nor wrong – they just ARE. Yes! They come from our culture, our system of beliefs, our past experiences and our education. They are defined very early in our lives, most certainly through the early childhood years, and remain as core principles for the ways in which we will behave and define ourselves throughout our lives.

Exercise (Part I)

I urge you to review the following table of values. Select between six and eight values that you consider to represent who you really are, i.e. the ones that define you. But let me add a footnote here – this is by means an extensive, nor exhaustive list. There may be many other values, not listed, that define your underlying principles. If the list in the table provided does not do you justice, I urge you to consider additional terms that better represent who you are.

Adventure	Happiness

Balance	Honesty
Caring	Independence
Challenge	Inspirational
Cleanliness	Integrity
Commitment	Kindness
Compassion	Love
Confidence	Passion
Courage	Patience
Creativity	Peace
Determination	Persistence
Excitement	Strength
Fairness	Truthfulness
Family	Vision
Fulfilment	Wisdom

Poland, T. (2008)

Identifying your core values is but a part of the journey to self-awareness required to understand the nature of your actions and behaviours. For example, my definition of INTEGRITY, may be completely different from another's definition. What I consider to be FAIR, may be entirely different from someone else's concept of fairness.

We therefore need to give animation or definition to what we understand to be the meaning of our values.

For example, three of my core values I have identified as:

Inspiration– Through right action, I act as an inspiration to others.

Commitment – I am unwavering in my commitment to what I believe and do.

Determination – I overcome obstacles.

You will see here that I have given 'life and meaning' to each of my stated values. I have *animated* the value by giving it a 'saying or meaning' that is very particular and pertinent for me.

Importantly, this is the meaning that the value has for me – not necessarily for anybody else.

Exercise (Part 2)

Having noted down your core values in Exercise I, I urge you now to give 'life and meaning' to each of the values that you have listed. Write a small caption, sentence or definition of what, for you, the value means.

Then, when you have done this, give yourself a pat on the back, for you have now defined, at your very core, who you are and what defines you. Remember, there is no 'right or wrong' or 'better or worse' with this exercise. It is purely an exercise of self-expression. It is a definition and appreciation of your true nature and an understanding of the source of your actions and behaviours.

A story: A Double-edged Sword

The samurai sword master was practising his skills one day. It was a fine day and there was a gentle breeze that caressed the cheeks of all who were in the vicinity of its graciousness. His practice was conducted in a field, just adjacent to the local village. A number of young children espied the sword master at his practice and came to sit and observe in wonder the sublime skills of the master swordsman. Truly, the master's skills were a sight to behold. There was a grace and serenity to each of his movements and the sword sung in the air as it carved a passage through the ether.

Finally, as the master stopped to wipe the sweat from his brow, one of the young children who was sitting in earnest observation, said to the master, 'Master, I bet you have killed many men with that sword?'

The master smiled at the eagerness of the young child and then said, 'Killed, young man? But I have not killed anyone, and certainly not with this sword. This is a sacred sword, handed down from the generations of my forefathers. It should not be tainted with the precious blood of man.'

'But master,' exclaimed the boy, 'as a master swordsman, surely your job is to rid the village of wrong doers and sinners. To kill your enemies and to rend them asunder with the power of your blade.'

'Yes, it is true, young man, that my skills as a sword master truly define who I am. I have spent many years practicing my skills with the blade to define the essence of who I am. Yet, it is what I do with these skills that determines my true merit in life.'

'Master,' said the young fledgling, 'I do not understand.'

'Young man, you see that my blade has two sides. One of these sides can be considered 'good', the other 'evil'. If I were to use the side that was 'evil', it would be to cause havoc and mayhem amongst my fellow men, I would kill and maim in the name of what I considered to be 'right'. I would cast out evil-doers and purge sinners in the name of a holy God. Yet, I choose to use the other side of the blade. This is the side that demonstrates, but does not inflict.'

'Master, what do you mean by 'demonstrates, but does not inflict'?'

'Young fellow, who would dare attack me, given the skills I have with this sword? Who would attempt to rob me or cause me harm, given the ease with which I can stop their attack? The essence of my strength lies, not in my ability to attack and destroy, but to deter and defend. This, as a master of the sword, is my greatest asset and that is the core and creed that I live by.'

'Master,' said another of the young children assembled at his feet, 'how do I become a sword master like you?'

'Young man, to be a role-model for you is an honour richly bestowed and humbly accepted. Come. The first lesson is here and now. You hold the blade like this ...'

... back to the pond

Monique had enough self-awareness to know that she needed help. The past days had been filled with such high levels of stress that she knew that her ability to function effectively was limited by anxiety. She needed release, she needed to unload the worry and pain, and she couldn't do that on her own But she knew who to turn to. It was then that her phone rang. It was Gabriel.

'You're an amazing man you know. You seem to have an uncanny knack of calling when I am most in need of your help. If you can ever explain to me how you do that, then I will be all ears.'

'Monique, it's no secret, but it is a mystery to many.'

'As always, my friend, you are full of the cryptic! I'll meet you at the old café next to the library in thirty minutes.'

'Okay, I'll see you there.'

On first glance, Gabriel could see that his friend had been through some challenging times and he invited her to offload all of the events that had transpired. It took some considerable time.

'Gabriel, you know, I really feel as if I'm being stretched to the limit with this whole affair and while I'm much closer to seeing the end, there seems such a long, and dangerous, way to go. But I just don't understand! Why in God's name would someone from the Brotherhood want to steal *The Book of Mysteries*?'

'In God's name is precisely the answer, Monique.'

'Why? What do you mean?'

'You and I both know that each and every being on this planet is a divine reflection of the most holy and that there are many pathways to experience that divinity. These philosophies, and more, are well expressed through the wisdom of *The Book of Mysteries*. Yet, its ideas challenge the established doctrines and beliefs that espouse a sole pathway to salvation.'

'Gabriel, I don't understand. What do you mean?'

'Many established codes of belief have their origins in the 'sacredness of their exclusivity'. In other words, they believe that their beliefs provide the one and only true pathway to redemption and the experience of the divine. They believe that following their code and system of belief is the only means by which a soul can escape the fear of purgatory or eternal hell-fire.'

'Okay, but that still doesn't explain why they should consider stealing what is, for many, a sacred relic of infinite wisdom.'

'Monique, if you understand the self-righteous fervour by which some of these organised religions proclaim the sanctity and exclusivity of what they believe, you will begin to unravel the reasons why they are able to justify all manner of abhorrent actions against the, so-called, non-believers.'

'But surely a book like *The Book of Mysteries* can do nothing to undermine the security of these established doctrines?'

'On the contrary, Monique, a book such as *The Book of Mysteries* does much to undermine such established doctrines.'

'Gabriel! But how?' enquired a bemused Monique.

'A book like *The Book of Mysteries* connects people to their ultimate truth. In other words, the words, stories and parables in a book such as this touch the heart so deeply that an individual's inner truth is deeply experienced. In other words, the individual can make an intimate connection with their God, without the need to rely on the presence of a 'so-called' intermediary, for example, a priest, imam, or a rabbi to facilitate the process, or tell them what to do and how to behave.'

'I see! So it is bad enough that the book espouses wisdom and doctrines that are not in accord with their system of beliefs. It is more that books, like *The Book of Mysteries*, make them somewhat redundant.'

'Exactly, Monique, exactly.'

Chapter 7

What you resist persists. Only what you hold can disappear.

... back at the pond

Given the magnitude of the information that Louise had received, it was no wonder that her mind was full of speculation. She knew that Horatio had been at the scene of the robbery of *The Book of Mysteries*. She also knew that he was a member of the Brotherhood of Ecumenical Light, and although she had seen the firebrand preacher —Brother Vladimir, she thought, was his name —she had no previous knowledge of any police matter that his group may have been involved in.

'What was the connection? Was there a connection at all?' she thought. She felt as if the mosaic was coming together. The only way to find out was to pay them a visit and, with this thought, she made an appointment to meet the head of the Brotherhood the very next day. But there was something wrong. Something was gnawing at her that she just couldn't put a finger on.

As she had done many times in the past, she immersed herself in the data and analytical aspects of the various crimes. She examined the pictures and turned the evidence over in her mind. Then it hit her. She knew what it was. At least, she knew now what she would do as her next move.

She went barging into the room of her superior officer and said, 'Captain, I need authority to conduct a phone tap.'

'For whom, and on what basis do you want this intervention?' said the Captain. 'Can't you get the evidence you need from some other, less aggressive form of policing?'

'Sir, I've found out that the duck that stole *The Book of Mysteries* is the same one that was found murdered the other evening out on the west side of the pond.'

'Hang-on a minute, Louise. I understand that all you found was a feather by the stand where the book used to sit. That doesn't mean that the previous owner of the feather is the same one that stole the book. Try and support that in court and we'll look like the keystone cops at amateur hour.'

'Yes sir, I know, but the fact is that the deceased was at the scene and was subsequently murdered. Then, we know the perpetrator went to great lengths to try to hide the poor chap's identity. This indicates to me that he was silenced for what he knew.'

'Louise, you haven't told me yet whose phone you intend to tap.'

'I want to bug the office of the leader of the Brotherhood of Ecumenical Light. I'm meeting him tomorrow to ask what he knows about the deceased, and about the theft of the book.'

Louise saw the face of her commander turn a lighter shade of pale.

'You've got to be kidding! Do you know how much clout that fellow's got? He's got a direct line to the Council of Elders who govern this pond. God knows, if it were ever uncovered that we bugged the phones of the Brotherhood, my arse would be pasted from Easter to Christmas time. Go and get me some solid evidence and maybe then I'll agree to put my head in a noose for you.'

… the next day:

Louise entered the grand chamber of the master of the Brotherhood of Ecumenical Light and whilst her demeanour was one of authority based on her position within the law, she was overcome by the sheer power of the man she was about to interview.

By the end of the discussion, though it came as no surprise, Louise was no further informed about either the murder of one of the Brotherhood's own members, or the possibility of his connection to the theft of *The Book of Mysteries.* She was, of course, emphatically urged to contact the order if she needed any further assistance.

Master Vladimir considered the interview to be at an end and stood up. Louise had no choice but to comply with the polite but firm hint to leave. She made her way out of the master's chambers and went out into the courtyard where she waited about ten minutes before putting the rest of her plan into action.

Running back into the antechamber to find the master's personal assistant, she breathlessly explained that she had left her handbag under the chair in the master's room and asked if she might go in and get it.

After a brief communication by the assistant on the intercom, she was invited to go in and collect her belongings.

'I'm dreadfully sorry, your grace, I am getting forgetful these days.' The master waved her away without so much as a glance and resumed his important considerations.

Once outside with some privacy, Louise removed the recording device from her handbag and pressed the rewind, then the play buttons. What she heard was the phone being picked up and the voice of Master Vladimir saying, 'Get me Barnabas Duck on the line.' The voice went on:

'Barnabas, in God's holy name, I've got a job for you and it needs to be done with summary execution. I expect you to be in my chambers in one hour.' Louise then heard the click of the phone being replaced on the receiver. The next voice she heard was her own, as she re-entered the chamber.

'Oh well,' she mused, 'Not exactly legal, but highly effective in the circumstances.'

Returning immediately to her office, she downloaded the details of said, Barnabas Duck, and the litany of what she saw made the colour blanch from her face. The next call she made was to Monique ...

Resistance is normal:

According to Wheeler (2007),

> Sadness, anger, frustration, resentment: these are all normal emotional states that must be allowed to come and go. Paradoxically, the more you try to deny your negative emotions, the more powerful they become, and the more stress they cause. ... A compelling thought or emotion will persist in its demand for attention until it's given its due. Only then will it lose its potency and fade away.

A tale of hot chips:

I was with my three sons some months ago and, as was their usual request, they wanted to enjoy a bowl of hot chips from their favourite local café. Now it must be said that their father is often averse to putting into the body, substances that are not that beneficial to one's wellbeing. But, truth be told, my resistance is often overcome when it comes to 'hot chips'.

Approaching the attendant, I requested a bowl of chips, but declined those that I observed in the food-warmer, as they looked as if they had been sitting there since time immemorial. So, I requested fresh ones. After we had sat down, the young attendant came up to me and, in a whisper said, 'Can you go and speak to the boss (nodding his attention to the lady behind the counter). She wants me to serve the old chips from the food-warmer. She'll get up me big-time if I don't.'

I glanced over at the 'boss-lady' and intuitively felt that she had an aggressive, stand-over type of personality. She looked as if she was used to getting her way through aggression and bullying.

'Sure,' I said to the young attendant.

I approached the boss-lady in a polite, but firm manner, in a style that bespoke a willingness to discuss the problem at hand.

'I requested a fresh plate of hot chips, rather than those in the display,' I said as I looked at her directly, 'Is this okay?'

She looked at me and sized me up for a moment, and then said, 'Sure.'

The main issue here is that 'what we create, we make real.' If we consider an issue to be monumental and overwhelming, then that is what it will be. This is what we have envisaged – so this is what we create. If we envisage something to be a problem, then it certainly will be one. If we fear something or someone, then that fear will be our reality. If I had considered the 'hot chip' request to be a problem, then I might have had some difficulty in finding a solution. I might have feared the boss-lady's aggressive nature and refrained from any intervention. I might have preferred to avoid any form of confrontation and accepted the 'week-old' chips from the food-warmer, or, I could have responded with in-kind aggression and demanded that my 'hot chips' be freshly presented.

The solution, whether it is for something as minor as the 'hot-chips', or a life problem eminently more profound, is firstly to *acknowledge* that the situation (or person) IS. This is not a judgement of 'good or bad' or 'pleasant or unpleasant'. It just IS. It doesn't mean that you agree (or disagree) with the situation, or the other's position. It merely means that you acknowledge it.

It can be acknowledged by noting 'how' that situation or emotion made you feel. For example, did you feel your muscles get tense? Which muscles? Did your heart rate increase, or your throat tighten-up in response? It can be acknowledged by observing 'what' actions it caused you to instinctively enable. For example, did you have an urge to 'leave the scene' (flight) or 'get stuck into them' (fight)? It can be acknowledged by observing 'how' you felt afterwards. Did you feel content with the way you acted, or regret that you acted in a certain way? How long did this feeling stay with you?

Once you acknowledge the situation, you can begin the process of *releasing* and this starts with the *breathing.*

In Chong (2011) I stated: "Breathing stimulates our lymphatic system and promotes the carriage of toxins from the body's cells. It decreases stress and increases energy; it assists in balancing the alkalinity and acidity of the body, and best of all … it's free."

Try the 7-1-7-1 exercise! Breathe in through the nose for seven seconds – hold for one second. Breathe out through the mouth for seven seconds – hold for one second. Repeat as often as necessary until equilibrium returns. Finally, you can now *release* the negative emotion (or stress) about this situation or event.

Repeat a little mantra, such as: "I am releasing the memory of this event out to the universe. I have no need of it anymore."

If you are a believer in God, then the mantra becomes: "I am releasing the memory of this event to you, God. I have no need of it anymore."

Remember: "Resistance is normal – whether we choose 'fight or flight', either way we make the situation real."

A story: There's No Fun Here

The diminutive old man was sitting on the park bench just feeding the gaggle of pigeons that had come along to share the crumbs from his lunch bag. It was a beautiful day and the sun was shining a treat. So much so that he had taken off his mantle and allowed the rays of the sun to work magic on his frail skin.

All of a sudden, he heard an approaching noise; a clamour of excessive banter and mockery was coming from a group of youths walking down the pathway.

From a distance the old man noticed that their attire seemed rather scruffy, but perhaps, he thought, this was just the way youngsters dressed nowadays. He paid them little attention and continued to feed the pigeons. Suddenly, and without seeking permission, one of the youths sat beside him somewhat rudely and encroached unnecessarily upon his personal space.

'Old man, what do you think you are doing?' he said, as he rudely knocked the bag of breadcrumbs from the old man's hands – much to the delight of the other youths.

'You must be well past the age when you can 'get it up anymore'. So I guess the only thing you have to look forward to in life is coming out here to feed the pigeons.'

Now, at this obvious provocation, the old man took a quiet and serene breath of fresh air and looked directly at his young antagonist.

'You are right young man, I do look forward to coming here and feeding the pigeons. But do you know why?'

'Why, old man? Please enlighten me?' said the young aggressor.

'Well, when I was younger, I had lots of misguided anger and aggression and it turned out that I hurt a lot of people.'

'So what? What does that have to do with feeding pigeons?'

'Well, it wasn't so much that I hurt a lot of other people. I paid my dues. But the twenty years I spent in prison were ultimately a waste of the most precious years of my life. Now, I find that I'm shunned by the people who had previously cared for me, and the only creatures that now give me unconditional love are these pigeons.'

'What a sob story, but what does that have to do with me, old man?'

'Nothing really, young fellow, except that you remind me of myself when I was your age, that's all.'

At these words, the young man's mouth fell open in gaping insolence and he stood up and said to his mates, 'Let's go. There's no fun here.'

The old man then rummaged in his sack for another bag of breadcrumbs and whistled to his companions to come back and resume their feast.

... and back to the pond:

'Monique, if you ask me how I came about any of the information I am about to give you, I'll clam-up and not say another word. Do you hear me?'

Louise settled into the chair next to Monique at their usual café.

'Okay, I agree,' was Monique's response to her friend's entreaty.

'There is a killer on the loose, who goes by the name of Barnabas Duck. He's got a rap sheet that would do justice to a child's wish list for Santa Claus. I also know that he's been charged with some divine task, assigned by His Grace, Master Vladimir from the Brotherhood of Ecumenical Light. I don't know what that task is, but given this duck's criminal history, it can't be good.'

Louise then passed across the table an envelope that contained a photo of the suspected perpetrator.

'Ahh yuck, a duck with a face that only a mother could love,' exclaimed Monique, 'but are you saying that this is the duck that committed that recent murder?'

'No, I'm not saying that. But that's only because I haven't got the evidence as yet. All that I'm saying is that this malevolent has been taken off his chain by his master and the outcome can't be good. I'm also saying that if you see this nasty little mongrel you'd better contact me straight away. His presence around you can't be a good sign.'

'Okay, I will, but Louise, I've got to tell you that I did pay a visit to Master Vladimir and I can assure you that I'll not be receiving a Christmas card from him this year.'

'Listen Monique, I know that we're both thinking along the same lines as far as these crimes are concerned, but more than that – I'm getting mighty concerned about your welfare. These boys are playing for keeps. Stay out of trouble; do you hear me? I'm protected by the authority of the law - but you, you stand out like a neon light on a dark night. For goodness sake be careful.'

'Yes, I will,' came the quiet response from Monique. 'But what do we have to do to catch these criminals, before someone else gets hurt and before *The Book of Mysteries* disappears forever?'

'I know what I'm going to do,' said Louise. 'I'm going to continue following the trail of evidence until I can nail these people. As for you, you are going to sit tight and keep your nose clean. Do you hear me?'

Yet, despite that ever-present sense of peril that clasped her stomach in a tight knot of fear, Monique knew that she would not rest until she had returned the book to its rightful place – that was her purpose.

... meanwhile, back in the chamber of the master of the Brotherhood:

'Barnabas, you are charged with another divine service in the name of Almighty God,' said Master Vladimir to his vassal.

'Yes your Grace. I am at the service of the Almighty and I am His willing servant.'

The master slipped an envelope across the table into the eager hands of the divinely inspired messenger.

'The photo of the duck in this envelope is that of a blasphemer and an apostate. Her very presence is an offence against God the Almighty and she must be disposed of in the usual manner.'

'Yes master, it will be done.'

'But Barnabas, be warned. There must be no trace of the body after you have fulfilled your divine purpose. The body must never be found. Do you understand me?'

'Yes master, all will be carried out according to your wishes.'

'Good, then make haste and may God give strength to your hand in performing its divine work.'

... at the same time:

Monique was lying on her bed trying to get some badly needed sleep, even if it were for just a few moments. But, alas, her mind was a turmoil of possibilities and ideas. The horrid face of the duck that Louise had shown her was an ever-present reminder to be careful. There was also a persistent fear that she acknowledged as a partner in her purpose to retrieve the sacred book. Yet, she had decided to allow this fear its expression by acknowledging its presence, at once, rather than allowing it to cause atrophy. She would use it to sharpen her senses and calculate the risks in her favour.

Slowly but surely, a plan formed in her mind and she jumped up from her bed and made a call to her contact at the Pond Post. She knew it was risky and dangerous, but it seemed to be the only way ...

Chapter 8

Tell your truth as soon as you know it, and as soon as you have an opportunity.

When I looked up the definition of 'truth' in the Oxford English Reference Dictionary (1995), it told me that truth is, "the quality of being true or truthful" ... a definition I find about as useful as a hole in the head. But no matter, I will persist. So, where else do I now turn but to the expressive explanations of ... Wikipedia, of course?

> ***Truth*** *has a variety of meanings, such as the state of being in accord with a particular fact or reality, or being in accord with the body of real things, real events or actualities. It can also mean having fidelity to an original or to a standard or ideal. In a common archaic usage it also meant constancy or sincerity in action or character. The direct opposite of truth is "falsehood", which can correspondingly take logical, factual or ethical meanings.*
> (http://en.wikipedia.org/wiki/Truth, accessed April 2011)

Oh boy! I've got to tell you ... I'm not much further ahead in my understanding of what truth is. Let's cast our net a bit further ...:

From *The Bhagavad-Gita as it is* (1984) we learn:

> *Just try to learn the truth by approaching a spiritual master. Inquire from him submissively and render service unto him. The self-realized souls can impart knowledge unto you because they have seen the truth.*

Sorry, but I'm still not there yet. I still don't get what truth is.

According to Meher Baba (1987) " ... *the divine Truths can start by hearing or reading expositions of the divine Truth, which have their source in the Masters of wisdom."*

Are we there yet?

Walsch (1998) says, "Yes, there is a One Great Truth; there is a Final Reality. But you will always get what you choose, regardless of that reality."

Later in the same book (1998) he says, "Ultimately, all real communication is about truth. And ultimately, the only real truth is love."

I must tell you, I think I'm getting there, but I'm still not sure that I've completely nailed it down! Okay, I will go looking some more …

Here we go. Once again Walsch (1997) comes to the rescue by stating:

> *The biggest lesson I have learned in my life revolves around truth. There is no such thing as Absolute Truth in the objective sense, but there is a subjective truth, there is what is true for you and that is extraordinarily important in your life.*

Okay, I'm getting it, but let's leave these definitions and discussions for now - my head is starting to hurt.

A story: Achieving your Goals

The young devotee sat at the feet of his master. It was time for their weekly discussions about life and a summing-up on the disciple's endeavours to dispel ignorance from his mind and install understanding. But on this particular day, the young man was sorely troubled.

'Master, I have been under your tutelage for some five years now. I have diligently studied all of the Holy Scriptures and can recite their divinity verbatim, and yet I feel no closer to my goal.'

'And what goal is that?' asked the master of his young charge.

'The goal of knowing what truth is,' said the disciple.

The master closed his eyes and seemed to withdraw into

himself to seek the answer to his disciple's conundrum. Finally, he opened his eyes and said, 'Young disciple, why do you seek truth as a goal?'

'Because, master, this is our reason for being. To seek ultimate truth through enlightenment and the wisdom of the ancients.'

'My son, why do you seek that which you already have?'

'But master, I do not understand. Surely truth is to be found only in the ancient scriptures and the holy writings.'

'My son, ultimate truth exists, but only in the realm of the absolute, where it cannot be experienced in the same way that life is experienced. The absolute is the home of your soul. In this life, you are in the realm of the relative, where your body and your mind take your soul upon its journey through the years. That is to say, your soul comes to know itself through your life's experiences. So, if you wish to find your truth, you must search within your own experience.'

'Master, I think I understand. But have we not been taught to place our trust in the Scriptures and the wisdom of the ancients?'

'Yes, this is so my son. This is what we have been taught for many centuries now. But do you think that God stopped talking to man all of those centuries ago? Can you imagine that all truth was given to man thousands of years ago, but has since ceased in its outpouring? I say to you that the truth you seek is within your heart. It is the divine connection between you and your God and requires none other than an open heart to allow it to come forth.'

'But master, what need then would I have of you as my master, or to read the Holy Scriptures?'

'My son, my role, like those of the ancient scriptures, is not to tell you your truth, but rather to shine the light on the pathway so you may see in which direction your own truth is to be found.'

... and we return to the pond:

Monique made contact with her colleagues at the *Pond Post* and told them she would be making a statement about *The Book of*

Mysteries and its whereabouts. She told them that she would be making the statement on the forecourt steps of the library at 3:00 p.m. the next day. And thus the first part of her plan was set in motion.

The next call she made was to the personal assistant to His Grace at the Brotherhood. However, before she made this call, she wrapped a cloth around the mouthpiece of the phone and deepened the pitch of her voice.

'Office of His Grace, Master Vladimir,' came the automated response.

'Tell His Grace that I know where the book is, and that if he values his reputation and that of his brotherhood, he had better watch the evening news on the television tomorrow night.'

'Who is ...?'

Click. Monique hung up before any further words could be spoken.

The next few hours were spent refining what she was going to say at the press conference the following afternoon. She also set up around her apartment the security apparatus that she had purchased the day before.

Finally, she made a call to Louise ...

'Louise,' she said, 'do you trust me?'

'Monique, I hate it when you start a conversation like that. Of course, I trust you, but I also know that you're like an unstoppable force heading towards an immovable object. What are you up to?'

'Sometime tonight you are going to be receiving a call from me. I don't know exactly when, I just know it's going to happen. When it does, I need you to be on my doorstep with at least three of your burly comrades at a rate reflecting the speed of light. Can you do that for me?'

'Monique, what in God's name are you cooking up?'

'Don't worry. Everything will be okay – just make sure that you turn up on time. Do you hear me?'

With her final job done for the day, it was time to allow her mind and tired body to experience a moment of peace. She curled up on her favourite cushion and began some breathing exercises that Gabriel had taught her. This allowed her to settle into a deep meditation.

By the doctrines:

"Then you will know the truth and the truth will set you free" –The Bible, John 8:32

A divine doctrine, like the one above, is not provided by the ancients because it represents some possibility or whimsical notion. Nor should it be acknowledged as a *doctrine of righteousness* that must be adhered to on pain of suffering, or worse — excommunication, persecution or purgatory. Divine wisdoms shine a light that allows our own truth to be revealed. They are guidelines for us to conduct our lives.

But we return to the problem at hand – what is 'truth'?

I understand that truth is provided in the ancient scriptures and doctrines, but I also understand that truth is not limited to these doctrines.

I also understand that I can learn the truth by listening to a master, a guru or a sage.

I also know that there is an *absolute* truth, but that this absolute cannot be experienced in the presence of duality. Let me explain. In life we exist within the laws of cause and effect, right and wrong, positive and negative. In other words we experience duality. However in the *realm of the absolute* there is no duality. Everything is perfect and part of the ideal. Think of the sun as the absolute and ourselves as filaments of the sun. The filament cannot know itself when it is bound within the whole. It cannot know who it really is. The filament can only become aware of itself experientially. In other words, it must choose to come to life to know itself, as if it were born anew into this world.

So, maybe the *right* question is, 'What is *my* truth?'

According to Griffiths (1978, 125), "To know things as they are, one must know one's self; one must go beyond sense and reason and know the Self in all things in the Self. This is wisdom, this is enlightenment, this is to know the Truth."

So, okay, we're moving this along – to the absence of ignorance. But let's take a little digression and discuss the word, 'know'.

In Chong, (2009, 108-109), I discussed the 'I AM' declaration. I stated that, "This 'I AM' declaration is so powerful and profound as to KNOW exactly who you are and what you do!"

I discussed this through the concept of 'levels of awareness'. These levels are:

- Hope (the first level), e.g. I *hope* that God exists.
- Belief (the second level), e.g. I *believe* that God exists.
- Knowing (the third level), e.g. I *know* that God exists. At this, the third level, we are absolutely clear that what we declare is true, or that it will happen. We have this clarity because we both *feel and experience* our truth.

The grand master, Jesus, said, "I am the way and the light." He did not say, 'I hope I am .... He did not say, 'I believe I am ...' He *knew.*

The origin, therefore, of MY Truth is *that which I feel and experience,* and therefore, *know* to be true.

A Story: The Robes of My Faith

A novice of the monastery had recently completed his devotions in the temple. He had prayed before the altar and obtained a blessing from the monk, before going about his chores of sweeping the courtyard and cleaning the chalice on the altar. Once these chores had been completed, the master monk gave permission for the novice to take some recreation in the village. This gesture, it must be said, was most rare given the strict regimen within the monastery.

Gleefully, therefore, the novice wondered down the road towards the village outskirts. His primary thoughts were to go and enjoy the hustle and bustle of the main centre square, where many goods were traded and bartered. As the day was particularly fine, he removed his hood to enjoy the slight breeze that caressed his face and cooled his forehead. Then, all of sudden, seemingly from nowhere, three youths came out from behind a bend in the road and started to menace and bully the novice.

'Well, look at what we have here,' said the first of the protagonists. 'It seems that we have one of those delicate little flowers from the monastery.'

'I wonder whether his God will save him from a beating,' said the second of the trio.

At this, the third of the group, gave the novice a solid whack to the head. The others hailed down numerous fierce blows and kicks upon the poor novice.

Lying battered and bruised upon the roadside, his head bleeding from a deep gash and his body bruised and aching from the kicks to his torso, the novice limped back to the monastery. Upon seeing his distressed state, the monk took the lad into the infirmary, tended to his wounds and gave him a delicious broth that would not only ease his pain, but also give him ease to sleep. Many hours later, when the young novice had awakened and broken his fast, the monk came to visit his young charge.

'How do you feel, young novice?' enquired the monk.

'Master, my body feels a little sore, but certainly, in time, these ills will pass.'

'Tell me the story and the events that lead up to this awful attack.'

So the young novice related the events as they had occurred, and the master monk pondered them with earnest attention and a stern gaze. Then the monk asked, 'And what of your spirit young man? How do you feel about what has happened to you?'

'Master, the three attackers took pleasure in their attack because I am different from them. In their ignorance they resort to violence to mask their own levels of fear and loneliness. I wear the robes of my faith and my actions testify to my belief in God. I know that God is in my heart forever. I know that wherever I go, so does God. Master, while my body has been bruised, it will recover. My heart, however, remains undisturbed in its radiance, for I know that God lives there.'

At these words, the master monk merely smiled deeply at the young novice, gave him a blessing, and returned to his duties within the monastery.

… let's go back to the pond:

Towards ten o'clock that evening, Monique felt that all was in readiness. She looked around her apartment, examined all the things she had put in place and could find nothing that she had missed.

Coincidentally, it was a dark night outside. The light of the moon was swathed in a heavy cover of mist and cloud, a portent of rain to come. Consequently, when she turned out all of the lights in the apartment, it was difficult to move around without stridently bumping into something.

She sat in the comfort of her lounge chair and waited …

Despite feeling a pinch of anxiety at the base of her stomach, she knew in her heart that this was the right course of action. Yes, it was risky, but she thought, anything worth striving for is worth a risk.

It seemed that the moments passed very slowly, and she had no idea what time it was when she heard a faint noise at the base of her front door. She heard the slight squeak of the door handle as it was turned, and the rustle of the lock mechanism as it was being prised open.

Her heart was beating at a mile a minute, but she refrained from jumping up from her seat, or making any noise, apart from her breathing … and then the door swung open.

She sensed the malice of the individual, even before she was aware of his physical presence.

'Come in, I've been waiting for you,' she said, as she flicked the switch by her chair and illuminated the room. What she saw made her take a quick gasp of air, for the hideous face of her would-be attacker looked almost serene in its desire to fulfil its 'divine' purpose. The light sparkled off the gilt edge of the hunting knife that he brandished in his hand.

'Barnabas, you have come to fulfil your 'divine' duties, I see. But why would you do this without first checking your actions with your God?'

'You are a blasphemer and an apostate, and it is my duty to see you cast into the fires of Hell where you belong,' said Barnabas.

'Yes, I understand you have been charged with a divine duty, but I ask you again. Have you checked with God?'

'Speak plainly woman, before I slit your throat, what do you mean, "Have I checked with God?"'

Monique felt the sweat trickle down her back and the saliva in her throat threatened to dry up – yet, she persisted.

'Well, before I take any significant action in my life, I check it through the "playback recorder".'

Barnabas, took a couple of steps towards Monique and in a voice full of menace said, 'I'm almost at the end of my patience with you and your measly words. I am going to give you one more chance to speak plainly before I carve the name of God in your chest.'

Monique, took a deep gulp of air to allow her nerves to settle and with all the strength she could muster, she refrained from picking up the taser gun that was secreted under her leg. Instead, she said, 'Barnabas, when I die and go to heaven, I know that I will sit with God and He will play back all of my thoughts, actions and deeds in this lifetime. He will replay for me all of the things that I have done to others and reveal to me how I made them feel by what I did to them, all the people I have hurt, all the people I have assisted. All will be remembered, all will be revealed.

Once this is done, God will say to me, "What you have done to your brothers and sisters, you have also done to yourself, for truly you are all one in the name of God the most holy. What you do unto others, you ultimately do unto yourself, in my Holy name. If you have killed and maimed – should you not feel their pain? If you have been malicious or violent – will you not endure the same suffering? What recompense will you make to those you have mistreated?"

'But … but, I have been a loyal servant to his Grace. I desire only to see my passage into the realm of paradise, in Heaven to sit beside God as His loyal servant.'

'Your actions have been sanctified by a duck who proclaims to know the will of God. Yet in his heart there lies only a hunger for power, an avarice for control and a will to dominate his fellow ducks. This cannot be the Will of God – this is not the place of pure love.'

'But … but, I have been a loyal servant to his Grace. I desire only to see my passage into the realm of paradise, in Heaven Ato sit beside God as His loyal servant.'

'And Barnabas, no more loyal a servant could a master desire than you to have by his side, but that master must speak the truth, not for his own benefit, but for the benefit of all others who are his brothers and sisters. The fact is that, in reality, the master is truly the servant.'

At these words, Barnabas sank to his knees and the knife made a sharp clang on the floor as it dropped from his palm.

'What have I done, what have I done?' he lamented. 'I have killed and caused so much pain to my fellow ducks. What am I to do? I will be cast into the pits of hell-fire for eternity for what I have done to my fellow ducks.'

'Barnabas, you cannot undo that which has been done, but you can start a new life in which you can speak your truth and serve your fellow ducks for the remainder of your days.'

'But how? You don't understand. If I do not fulfil my duties to his Grace, I will be hung, drawn and quartered. My life will be forfeit, and even if I do manage to evade his wrath, I am a criminal and will be cast into prison for all the foul deeds I have committed.'

'Barnabas, you must speak your truth. This will be your redemption. You know that the Bible said, "Speak the truth and the truth will set you free." Make this your new beginning - your start to a new relationship with your God. You no longer need to be the servant of a false man. Rather be a servant to your own God. You can start now; you have no time to waste.'

Barnabas started to cry and his tears were near limitless. Then, after such lament, he took his cloak and wiped the snot and spittle from his face, making the queasy feeling in Monique's stomach almost reach the point of revulsion. Yet she persisted.

'Barnabas, if you are willing, I can start you on this new beginning. It will be for you then to forge your own pathway in the life ahead.'

'But what must I do?'

'I am going to call a friend of mine, from the police force ...'

'But they will arrest me ...'

'Barnabas, this cannot be avoided, but they will protect you. Then tomorrow, you will stand beside me, on the steps of our library, and there you can speak your truth. You can tell all that his Grace has made you accountable for. It is then that you will begin your new relationship with God – you will be renewed. Are you ready and willing?'

Barnabas was a mass of tangled emotions, but he managed to mumble a 'Yes, I am ready'. Then Monique made the phone call to Louise ...

When Louise arrived with her three assisting officers,

Monique pressed into her palm the tape recording she had made of the recent events.

'This will explain all you need to know. Just make sure he is ready to stand next to me at the press conference tomorrow afternoon.'

After they had all left, Monique closed the door behind her. Immediately, she sensed the absolute quiet of her living room. Then the strength in her legs gave way and she fell to her knees in total and utter exhaustion.

Chapter 9

What we cause to effect in others, we ultimately experience ourselves

In my life I have undoubtedly caused others to experience a multitude of different feelings and experiences. Without doubt, I have caused people pain, emotional and also physical perhaps. Without doubt, my actions and behaviours have caused others to feel anger, remorse, sadness and distress. Yet, it is also true that my actions and behaviours have caused others to feel elation, happiness, glee and comfort.

To be sure, I am sometimes aware of the feelings I create within another person, but often I am completely unaware of the effect my actions or behaviours have had or are having on another human being.

The list of our relations and interactions with others would be gigantic if we were to assemble them on a time-line. It would be impossible to contemplate if we attempted to consider each of them individually. To consider all of our effects on others over a lifetime spanning multiple decades would be mind-boggling.

Simplicity returns to some extent if we can limit our perspective to the individual reactions and interactions that may occur, say, between a husband and a wife, or a parent and a child. But what if we consider the multiple interactions elsewhere, say in the social arena or the workplace? What about those between a director of a company and a group of its employees? How about a politician and a group of constituents? How about a preacher and a congregation? The influence, in these circumstances, of the one upon the many is considerable indeed. Single individuals, through their actions and behaviours, cause a multitude of others to feel and experience a vast array of feelings and responses, ranging from the sublime and the harmonious to the disastrously painful and distressful.

Take Adolf Hitler as an example. The actions of this one man of historical and political prominence visited such an excess of pain and suffering upon millions and millions of others that the vastness of those effects cannot reasonably be grasped by the human mind. Yet, he certainly did these things and his actions did have those consequences. Back in the 1930s and 1940s his actions were abhorrent to the sensibilities of human kind, they remain so to this day and they will be just as abhorrent in the future. Within any moral framework devised by humankind, the effect of his actions upon others, in and after his lifetime, can only be described as abominable.

The Johari Window

The Johari Window as explained by Luft and Ingham (1955) is a cognitive psychological tool that was created to help people understand their interpersonal communication and relationships.

According to Cole (2001), "It shows two dimensions to understanding ourselves:

1 aspects of our behaviour and style that are *known* or *not known* to us (*self*); and
2 aspects of our behaviour and style *known* or *not known* to those we have contact with (*others*)."

This is depicted in the following model as figure 1, opposite.

The area identified as the *arena* represents information that everybody knows. For example our name and certain personal details such as place of employment, or career credentials. Interestingly, with the advent of the internet and on-line social media such as Facebook and Twitter, the depth and breadth of this information is far greater than ever before. The *arena* also represents personal actions and behaviours that are overt and

Johari Window

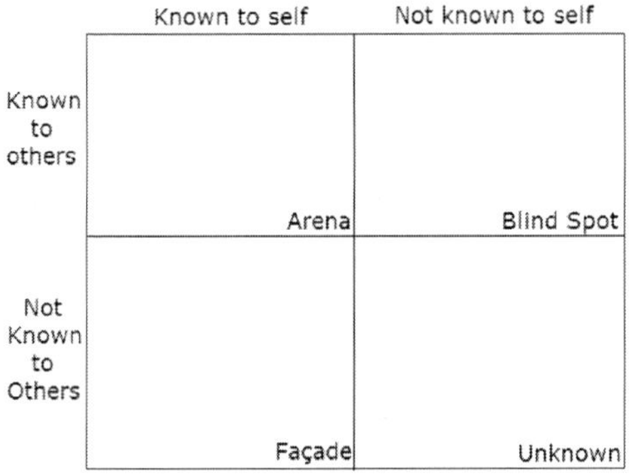

intentional. For example, we may deliberately be nasty to someone and cause them grief or emotional pain. An intentional act of violence on our part may cause visible physical harm.

The area identified as the *façade* (or sometimes the *closed area*) represents the area of secrets, that which we know about ourselves, but do not disclose to our friends, acquaintances or peers. This area has much to do with our thoughts and feelings, particularly those that we do not willingly articulate or express.

The area identified as *blind* represents the aspects of ourselves that others are aware of, but of which we ourselves remain oblivious. This may be a matter of mannerisms, or communication style or personal habits. The *blind area* also has impact upon others. We perform our actions upon and behave towards others, but at the same time we are totally oblivious of the effect we are having upon them.

The last area, identified as *unknown,* demonstrates information that is unknown to others, as well as to the self. This could typically be identified as the domain of the sub-conscious, or of dreams.

What is relevant to note about the Johari Window is the relative size of each quadrant. In the model above, each quadrant is depicted as having the same size, but, in reality each of these quadrants will be of differing dimensions for each individual person. Some people will have a large *arena* and, perhaps a small *closed* area. Others will have completely different Johari window characteristics.

A story: Good Deeds

The wise old master was sitting on his meditation mat in the main hall of the temple. The day was chilly and the old man felt the age of his bones even though he wore a woollen cloak to keep out the cold. Yet, despite the discomfort, he felt at peace with himself and his surrounds.

All at once a number of young boys, novices to the temple, came scampering into the hall in playfulness and joy. It was the time they most loved, for they got to sit at the feet of the wise old master and speak with him about many things on the subject of life and the wider universe.

'How are you today, my young charges?' the master asked the young lads.

'We're fine, thank you master,' came the collective response.

'And what would you like to speak about today?' the master enquired of them.

One of the young lads had a quizzical expression on his face as he put up his hand in response to the master's question.

'Yes, young man, what is on your mind today?'

'Master, I have heard it said by some of the other monks that the reason we should do good deeds here on earth is that this will open the doors when we go to Heaven. But what of all of the other things that we do in our life? I mean a lot of the things we do affect others, but we are unaware of what we have caused them to feel and experience? What if I do bad things to others without intending or meaning to?'

The old master looked closely at the young novice and observed the wisdom and potential of the young man in his care. Then he shut his eyes, as if in deep meditation.

After what seemed an eternity, the old master spoke.

'My sons, I am a very old man now and soon I will pass on to the next realm that awaits me, Heaven. Yet, I will do this without fear or trepidation. I will embrace with open arms the experiences that await me on the other side of the veil. But, the question is, how is it that I can embrace this transition without any fear?'

'I don't know,' came the response from the young man.

'In my life, I have done many things and experienced a multitude of passions, pains, sorrows and joys. Yet, I cannot know what is good or right for another. I can only speak my own truth and follow my own heart as it was right and good for me.'

'But master,' came the entreaty, 'how are we then to know what is right and good for our fellow man? Surely, the job of a monk is to do good deeds for others so that they may have a more pleasant life?'

'Young novices, I tell you truly that what you do to and for others on earth, you will surely experience in the love of the next realm. For in truth, what you do to others, you also do to yourself - for in the realm of Heaven, we are all one. Those whom you see as separate beings here on earth, are as one in heaven.'

'But master, I say again, how can we know if that which we cause in others is good and right?'

'Young man, the reason I have no fear of moving to the next realm is because I have lived by a simple motto, which is:

"Do unto others only as you would do unto yourself."

This motto is the great enabler to a life without fear of reprisal or consequence, for I would only do those things that I myself would treasure and enjoy. If you too can live by this motto, then you too, like me, will live a life of joy, happiness and liberation from fear and trepidation.'

'I charge you now with some homework, my young novices. For the next twenty days, when you look at or interact with another human being, you are to see them as if you are looking at yourself. If you do that, all of your actions and deeds will be directed through the passion for and respect of the self. Then, after the twenty days, you are to return to me and tell of all your experiences and questions.'

... and we return to the pond:

It was nine o'clock in the morning when Louise and Monique entered unannounced into the antechamber of his divine Grace, Master Vladimir from the Brotherhood of Ecumenical Light.

'You can't come in here unannounced,' said the perplexed and chastened personal assistant.

'Silence! If you say another word, I'll have you arrested for obstruction of justice,' said Louise as she flashed the badge of her authority at the now contrite secretary.

Glancing at Monique, she said, 'No more than ten minutes, as we agreed.' At the same time Monique, opened the double doors that led to the office of his divine grace.

What she saw initially took her by surprise, for Master Vladimir was prone on the ground, prostrate before the huge symbol of his God that hung from the wall of his chamber. By some quirky movement of the early morning light, a ray of golden orb seemed to surround the emblem of faith as it shone, divine and luminescent from the heavens.

The visage that confronted Monique, as Master Vladimir raised himself from his prone position, was measurably different from the mask of power and dominance that she had encountered on her last visit to his chamber. What she saw this time was a face in desolation. A palpable sense of impoverishment emanated from every pore on the face of this once-powerful chief of his brotherhood.

'Master Vladimir, what do you seek when you now pray to your God?' enquired Monique assertively.

In a voice now devoid of its previous authority and assuredness, Master Vladimir answered, 'All of my life I have sought to serve Almighty God. I have striven to fulfil the words of the Holy Scriptures in the lives of all ducks, that they may enter the gates of heaven on the wings of the holy angels. And now, now ... now I am cast adrift and to be persecuted for fulfilling the word of God. Why? Why has God given me this poisoned chalice?'

'Yet,' retorted Monique, 'in the name of everything you consider holy, you have committed some egregious crimes against your fellow ducks. You have ordered and visited pain and suffering upon members of your own flock. How can you justify these actions in the name of God?'

'My task was always to defend the righteous seekers of the one true way to God in Heaven. I was charged by God himself to bring seekers of the one-truth to His doorstep.'

'And as for those that you considered apostate or non-believers, you deemed it expedient to harm and destroy them!' retorted Monique.

'It was I, and I alone that was charged with this holy mission. God gave me the voice and the power to bring the sinners to him for redemption. Those that did not believe were merely lost souls, to be condemned to the fires of Hell for all of eternity.'

'And what of you Master Vladimir? When it is your time to pass from this world and face your God, what will He say to you?'

Tears then sprang to his eyes and he was speechless for some considerable time. It was as if a tsunami-like wave of emotion had engulfed this once powerful duck, in a deluge of divine retribution.

' ... I am forsaken,' was all he could manage to whisper.

'Yes, but are you sorry?' demanded Monique.

'How can I be sorry for being the instrument of the word of God?' he said with a glimpse of defiance. 'What of the many hundreds of souls I have saved from eternal damnation? Those many that have been redeemed from destitute lives that knew not the love of God?'

'And why do you think that God needed your help to save

these souls?' retorted Monique.

'Because I am his holy messenger, you God-forsaken sinner,' shouted Master Vladimir as he slammed his wing onto the nearby desk.

Monique, unruffled by this outburst, said, ' … and yet you pray to your God seeking absolution from your sins, only to find a deafening silence in response.'

'Master Vladimir, although, in your eyes, I am a non-believer, I neither condone, nor condemn what you have done. But do you believe in 'justice reinvestment'?'

'What do mean, 'justice reinvestment'?'

'Well, your grace, it is a well-established fact that the greater the degree of social inequality within a community of ducks, like our own, the greater the level of crime and the consequent demand for punitive justice. Justice reinvestment is a society's way of spending money *in* the community, not *on* it. It is a means of dealing with social problems, not just criminal justice.'

'Yes, well, what does this have to do with me?'

'Well your Grace, you are going to be given the opportunity to stand by me this afternoon along with your previous vassal, Barnabas, and confess to your crimes against members of this community. There you will have the opportunity to commence your process of redemption, by diverting funds from your Brotherhood and committing these funds to creating greater equality within our community of ducks.'

'Perhaps, just perhaps,' continued Monique, 'you might redeem yourself in the eyes of the community and the law, and thereby gain a reduced period of incarceration.'

'Oh and one last thing, Your Grace. Before you are taken into custody - do you believe in "divine intervention"?'

'Of course I do! I have lived by this creed all of my life.'

'Good! Then go and retrieve *The Book of Mysteries* and we will put this firmly to the test, shall we.'

Master Vladimir then proceeded to the northern side of his

office and there removed a large holy picture from the wall. What was then revealed was a secreted wall-safe to which he applied a combination and key. As he removed the sacred text, Monique's eyes widened and her heart skipped a small beat at the sight of the treasured tome, intact and undefiled.

'Good. Thank you, Your Grace. Now place the book on your desk and open it at any page you like.'

Master Vladimir did as he was instructed. All of a sudden, the ray of golden light that had previously illuminated the wall and its sacred symbol suddenly moved and fell upon the sacred text on the desk. Coincidentally, without any breeze or physical assistance, the pages of the sacred book started to flutter of their own accord. Then, as if by magic, they settled at an open page.

Without looking at the text and remaining firmly attentive to Master Vladimir, Monique said, 'Now read to me what is written on this page.'

Master Vladimir looked at the page that remained open on the desk. As he did so, his lower lip started to quiver and his face contorted into a paroxysm of grief and pain.

Then, through whispered breath, he said, 'All it says is ...

"God does not need your help."'

Thereupon the doors to the chamber burst open and Louise marched in and arrested Master Vladimir.

Consequences:

According to Walsch (2002):

> When you do the thing called "die" – that is, after you end your time with a physical body here on Earth – you will be given the opportunity for a Life Review. In fact, you will ask for it ... During this Life Review you will be allowed to experience every moment of your life, everything that you ever thought, said or did ... You will not only experience it from your point of view, you will experience it from the point

of view of every person whose life you touched.

I do believe this leads us to a Golden Rule:

"Do unto others only as you would do unto yourself."

Chapter 10

Disentangle yourself from the unacceptable and pursue with determination what matters most.

The mere setting of a goal will not ensure its realisation. Creatively visualising an outcome will not guarantee its success. Using affirmations to re-programme the sub-conscious mind is a highly effective way of conceiving an improved lifestyle or mindset, but it is not an assurance that our experiences will be dramatically altered.

In order to realise a more fulfilling life and create enhanced experiences, goal-setting, visualisation and affirmations are highly valued tools at your disposal. Yet, the missing link in each of these strategies is the effective alignment between the end-result (or outcomes) you want, and your actions (or inputs). In essence, this means that there has to be a dedicated investment of time for each outcome-related input.

By way of example, you may set a weight loss goal - to lose ten kilograms in two months – a realistic and achievable goal, to be sure. You can envision yourself in a set of new clothes that have long been your aspiration. You can reaffirm positive affirmations of self, such as, "I am worthy", or, "I love myself". Each of these is an important part of the process, but there must be an allocation of time that is scheduled each day, so that your actions (inputs) support the achievement of the goal. You could, for example, reshape your diet to reduce your intake of calories or sugars. You may conduct an extended exercise regimen or spend time cooking a nutritious and balanced meal, rather than buy a take-away full of sugars, preservatives and processed fats.

The key is to *schedule* time (daily) for the required inputs, so that the desired results (outputs) will be realised.

A Story: A Double-edged Sword (cont.)

This is the continuation of the story from Chapter 6 …

Both the sword master and his new apprentices wiped the sweat from their brows after the first arduous lesson of swordsmanship. The lesson was long and required the young novices to exercise muscles that had previously remained dormant and under-utilised.

'What do you think of the first lesson?' enquired the master, after they had quenched their thirst.

'Well Master,' said the first of the team, 'I'm tired, but I'm ready and willing to undertake more lessons. But tell us Master, how long will it take before we can each be considered masters of the blade?'

'Young novice, I have been practicing my craft, a little each day, for the past fifteen years.'

At these words, the master heard an involuntary gasp from the second member of the troop.

'And what ails you, my young novice?' enquired the master.

'But Master, how am I ever going to practice these skills every day for the next fifteen years? I have so many things to do. I have to go to school and do my homework. When I get home my parents make me do chores around the house. Then, when all of these things are done, I'm usually too tired to lift my head from my pillow and I go to sleep.'

The master pondered these problems for a moment or two before he responded.

'Young novice, how important is becoming a sword master to you? Are you truly passionate about it?'

'Yes, master, I am, but how I'm ever going to find the time to practice, I truly do not know.'

'Young man, I want you to think back to what you did yesterday and answer this question. How much time did you spend in activities that were purely for your amusement and entertainment?'

'Well master, I spent forty-five minutes watching the games in the village. I also spent thirty minutes playing sport with my friends. I also did not raise myself from bed until 7.30 am because I was so tired.'

'So, my young novice, if you spent only thirty minutes watching the village games and maybe played sport for only fifteen minutes, and if you got out of bed at 7 o'clock, rather than 7.30 am, you could rightly spend one hour in sword practice, could you not?'

'Yes master, but surely we have to have some fun in our lives? We can't be practising every day!'

'My son, if you truly desire to become a grand sword master, if this is your passion and committed purpose, then the reallocation of these activities will not be important. You see, they do not take you towards your goal. When you become a true master of the sword you will view these distractions as a butterfly would view the earth-bound progress of a caterpillar.'

'Therefore,' said the master, now addressing the entire group of young aspirants, 'are you ready to continue?'

'Yes we are Master,' they cried in unison.

... let us return to the pond:

Assembled at the steps of the pond's library was a mass of reporters from a vast array of television, radio and print media. There must have been over one hundred representatives of the press, each vying for the most advantaged spot to obtain an interview or ask a question. Behind this throng of eager humanity was a plethora of cables, relays and electronics that would link the pending moment to the rest of the world with the instantaneous press of a button.

As the third hour of the afternoon approached, Monique stood on the foyer of the library, flanked by her two recent antagonists, namely Barnabas Duck and his Grace, Master Vladimir. Both Barnabas and Master Vladimir were manacled on either side to a burly member of the constabulary.

It was a warm day and despite a gentle, cooling breeze, the perspiration and tension on the faces of the two accused felons was plain for all to see. On a table, directly behind Monique, stood a package, wrapped in silken cloth, which was obviously going to be the principal topic of the press conference. She began …

'Ladies and gentleman of the media, I have called this press conference to announce to you all that the prized possession of our humble library has now been returned to its rightful place. It is back here in the library. As you are all aware, *The Book of Mysteries* was the founding manuscript of our world-renowned library. It represents the cornerstone of our knowledge and of our cultural and spiritual life, and it is a central pillar of our library's very existence.'

As she said these last words, Monique turned to the table located behind her and removed the silk cloth covering the sacred text.

'Ladies and gentleman, as you can see the text remains intact and undefiled, a gift for which I am eternally grateful. It has been my dedicated purpose over these past months to see the book returned to its rightful place, and now this mission has been accomplished.'

A collective round of applause burst from the gathered media, but Monique held up her palm to request silence so she could continue.

'Over this same period, there has been much speculation in the media about the theft of our treasured manuscript and its link to some most unfortunate and heinous crimes within our community of ducks. However, it is not for me either to condemn or condone these acts of lawlessness; rather it is my choice to offer an opportunity to those accused to make declarations of redemption. Thus they may prepare not only their own pathways to a renewed life, but also, and more particularly, the opportunity for the current and future generations of our pond's community to prosper and improve. I will now hand the microphone to the first of the accused, Barnabas Duck.'

Truly, you could have heard a pin drop. There was absolute silence amongst the gathered media representatives – a feat not routinely achieved at such a gathering.

'My name is Barnabas and I have committed some terrible sins against members of our community. However, I did this because I believed I was divinely instructed to fulfil the will of God here at the pond. I feared the loss of my immortal soul if I did not carry out those tasks. Now, of course, I am well aware that this fear was misguided and untrue.

I am ready to receive my punishment, but I am also ready to serve my community and fellow ducks in whatever way will bring benefit and wellbeing, particularly to those in need. Therefore, if I am to be condemned as a criminal, please give me the chance to redeem myself through good works.'

' … and why should we?' came an angry voice from the back of the media scrum.

Then, without hesitation, Barnabas replied, 'I guess it's because I am a sinner, just like you.'

… and you could still hear a pin drop.

Monique then said, 'I will now hand over to his Grace, Master Vladimir from the Brotherhood of Ecumenical Light.'

'I am Master Vladimir, leader of the Brotherhood of Ecumenical Light and I have lived in passion for my God for all of my life. Through my good works and heavenly brotherhood, I have brought many souls to the pathway of righteous living. Yet, in doing so, I myself have strayed from the path. I too have committed crimes against my fellow ducks, for what I believed was a righteous cause.

I cannot undo what I have done, but I can make restitution for the crimes I have committed. This said, I will donate one million dollars to the community to be used for the reduction of social inequality within our society, and to reduce the level of crime amongst our poor and underprivileged.'

Then another voice sounded clearly from the middle of the assembly. 'You only give back money that was given to you by ducks from within our community. Why should such money be a cause for your redemption ... are you trying to buy our favour?'

For a moment Master Vladimir hung his head and it was obvious that he was struggling to retain his dignity and once mighty self-respect.

'Like Barnabas, I cannot undo what I have done. I can however use the resources at my disposal to benefit our society.'

'But you do not give of yourself, you only give what rightfully belongs to others,' came the same voice from the crowd.

'I am ready to receive whatever punishment is deemed for my crimes, but I also stand ready to give back to the community whatever service I can render that will bring peace and prosperity to the multitude of lives within the pond.'

At these words, a sea of hands shot into the air and a hundred voices spoke in unison asking a whole gaggle of questions. It was impossible to hear one from the other.

'Ladies and gentlemen, ladies and gentlemen,' shouted Monique assertively as she tried to bring a semblance of quiet to the assembled group, 'if I can have your attention for just a few moments longer.'

'It was not my intention to bring these two ducks before you so that there could be a trial by media. That is not my job, neither is it yours. Therefore I will not allow them to be questioned. Rather they will be returned into custody and the full processes of jurisprudence will be allowed to take their proper course.'

As she said this, she nodded to the attending constables to take the accused back to holding cells to await judgement and sentencing. To the assembled media, she then said, 'I am however happy to take a question or two.'

At this, the noise level increased exponentially as a thousand questions came tumbling towards the director of the library who now felt herself to be under siege. Completely at random, Monique chose one of the reporters in the front row.

'How do you feel about all that you have been through in the past few months? Are you happy that it's all over?'

Monique pondered these questions for a moment and then said, 'I will answer your second question first.'

'Am I happy that it's now all over? I am absolutely bloody ecstatic that it's all over and that our treasured manuscript has been returned to its rightful place. This was my purpose all along. As to your first question, these past few months have been, without a doubt, the greatest trial of my life. I have done things that have challenged me to the limits of my capabilities. Yet, I stand in wonder at what these challenges have brought out of me. If I had not been faced with these challenges, I would never have known what I was capable of. I now know that I am capable of achieving much more than I could ever previously have conceived ... even in my wildest dreams.'

There was another gabble of questions from the media throng, and Monique, again at random, chose another reporter, this time from the back of the group.

'And what are you going to do with yourself now?'

At this question, Monique's smile was like a beacon of light.

'Firstly I am going to take a well earned vacation, then ... then I, umm, maybe ... Actually, I really don't know what I'm going to do,' she exclaimed. 'And you know what? It actually doesn't matter. Thank you for attending, ladies and gentlemen.'

Monique then picked up *The Book of Mysteries* and quickly made her way directly into the library for a few moments of peace and reflection.

Phrases for disentanglement:

I trust that these phrases for disentanglement (in life) will serve you well:

- The idea that there is not enough time in a day is a fallacy. It is not possible to create more time, but you can cut down on the activity you put into the time that is there.
- Do only those things that represent your highest good.
- Prioritise your activities as important and/or urgent: that way you will know what to do first.
- If you cannot change your actions or your thinking, be prepared to obtain the same results as you always have in the past.
- 80 per cent of your current results in life come from 20 per cent of your actions (Pareto Principle) – so you need to be really clear on what the 20 per cent is, and then do more of it.
- Schedule time in each day to think.
- To think clearly and be creative you have to stop being so busy.
- Make an escape from responsibilities that you have allowed others to impose upon you and that take away your precious time.
- Have more fun and less stress.
- Laugh more than you currently do.
- Do not equate your sense of self worth with how hard you work; rather attach your worth to how you benefit others.
- Refrain from creating complexity in your life – this is a bureaucratic function.
- Learn from your mistakes; they are generally your best teachers.
- If something is not working, don't keep doing it.

Chapter 11

What would love do next?

A story: The Mistress's Anguish (cont.)

This is the continuing story from Chapters Four and Five ...

It was some three weeks later, after the letter had been sent, that the Mother Superior received the high-level delegation that had been dispatched from the central prelate under the direct orders of her Divine Mistress, the leader of the order – she who was acknowledged to be the greatest orator of her faith

While the mistress of the abbey was aware of the purpose of this high-powered visit, it did set many tongues wagging amongst members of the clergy and the mistress's followers. There was one, however, who knew of the reason for the visit and this knowledge made the young novice extremely anxious and concerned. Her concern was for the well-being of her mistress and for the future of the abbey that she had called home for these many years past. Despite her anxiety, the young girl was not going to await any official proclamations, or decrees. She was not willing to 'go down without a fight', so, without further ado, she set about doing what she thought was right and true.

Meanwhile, the high-level delegation got straight down to business and called the mistress of the abbey to a meeting that was to decide its fate and hers. Of course, the meeting was held behind closed doors, well away from the prying eyes and ears of the other members of the abbey.

Not much is known about the substance of the meeting. What is known, however, is that the participants were sequestered in the room for over four hours and periodically, despite the closed doors, raised voices could be heard through the walls and passageways.

In the meantime, the young novice set about knocking on as

many doors of the village as she possibly could. As she knocked on each door, her message was the same, 'Our mistress and our abbey are in trouble. You must come to the abbey right away - you must tell others.'

And so it was that the few told the many, and soon over a thousand village folk were assembled in the abbey's forecourt and outside its walls. There was barely a space for people to move, yet all that they knew was the message they had been told. There was a great unease, even a malaise, in the air.

Finally, the mistress and the official delegation emerged from the room after many hours of bitter debate. The mistress herself, while regal of stature, looked as if the weight of the world had been placed on her shoulders. It must be said also, that the members of the delegation also looked haggard, as if they had gone fifteen rounds with a prize-fighter.

As the mistress walked from the chamber and onto the balcony to take some fresh air, the sight that confronted her made her heart skip a beat and swell with pride. The stunned look on her sallow face told the crowd all they needed to know.

'Mistress, what ails you? What have these people done to you? What do they want?' came the ardent questions from amongst the assembled villagers and members of the abbey.

'My children,' said the mistress, 'my heart is gladdened by the presence of each of you here today. But my heart is also heavy, for I have some distressing news that I have been commanded to relay to you.'

'No!' came a chorus of many voices in unison.

But the mistress held up her hand for silence.

'By decree of the most revered Mother Superior of our order, our abbey is to be closed down ...'

At these words there was a great outcry and hullabaloo. The level of anger in the crowd rose exponentially, but once again the mistress held up her hand for silence and calm.

'My children, over these past years I have shared with you

many of your trials and tribulations, as well as many of your triumphs and treasured moments. It is now time for me to retire from the active service of the order to which I have devoted my entire life.'

Yells and tears of anguish broke out in the crowd of villagers. There were a great many disgruntled shouts of humbug and derision levelled towards the members of the delegation, who interestingly had sought refuge inside a room of the abbey, out of sight of the crowd. Then, all of sudden, a high pitched voice could be heard coming from a window in the top corner of the building, just to the right of the balcony from which the mistress had made her address. It was the young novice, the one that had encouraged the villagers to assemble as they had.

'Good people of the village,' she proclaimed, 'do you want this injustice to continue?'

'No!' was the collective roar.

'In the name of all that is holy, do you want the abbey to be closed and the village to be left without its spiritual support?'

Once again, 'No!' was the collective response.

'Well, in the name of all of the people assembled here, I propose that we present our views to these members of the delegation who are, as we speak, sheltering within the abbey. I want five of our village elders and community leaders to come forth now and speak to this delegation and tell them how we feel. What do you say?' she asked the mass of assembled villagers.

'Aye, let it be so,' was the collective response.

... and so it was that five village elders and community leaders came forth from amongst the crowd and made their way into the abbey's sacred inner hallways.

Then the young novice continued, 'I want the rest of you here to pray. To pray as hard as you can to your God, that your abbey may be saved and our beloved mistress may remain as leader of her flock.'

At these words, many fell to their knees in supplication to the Almighty. Many were the shrill tears and wails of lament that rang out to the sky and many were the rich baritone voices of the men who chanted in favour of the plea.

Now, the historical records of the meeting between the appointed members of the village and the delegation are limited. They shed a very dim light on the proceedings of the second meeting. That meeting also lasted many hours and when the participants finally exited the room, their bedraggled look bespoke long and hard negotiations.

The two delegations moved onto the balcony to address the assembled crowd. It was almost as big as ever. Only a few of the old and infirm had retired to their homes. The crowd stood as one, as a designated member of the village delegation cleared his parched throat to address his people.

'By the grace of the revered Mother Superior of our order, it is now decreed that your abbey will remain open for a period of six months henceforth. However, during this period of six months your abbey must receive a minimum amount of donations into its funds, and the numbers of your brethren supporting the abbey must increase by an amount stipulated in the agreement. If these conditions are not met, your abbey will still be closed at the end of the sixth month period. It is also decreed that during this period, your abbey will continue to be governed by your current leader, its present mistress.'

An almighty cheer cascaded from the combined voices of the crowd. It lasted many minutes, and there were boundless tears of joy and gratitude to the God who had answered their prayers.

After a short while, the mistress of the abbey moved forward to address the crowd. This is a transcript of what she said.

'My sons and daughters, I am greatly humbled by the might of your voice that has saved our abbey from extinction. We *will* make these targets that have been set … we have much work to do … but we *will* make them through the sweat of our brows and the grace of our God who gives strength to our hearts.'

At these words, a cheer arose from the assembly, but the mistress raised her hand to request silence. She continued:

'What we know is that in the heart of each man, woman and child assembled here today is a little piece of our abbey's life, and we will not rest in our efforts to ensure that its treasured service to you, the villagers of the community, continues well into the future. But, what I say to you most earnestly is that you must learn the greatest lesson of today.'

'And what is that?' came an entreaty from amongst the crowd.

'Our greatest lesson today is that such a tiny voice, from the most inconspicuous amongst us, can have such a profound impact on the lives of a multitude of others.'

At these words, she pointed towards the young novice who was standing fixedly on the sidelines, in awe of her mistress's words.

'The determined and passionate voice of this young novice has saved this abbey. It is she who should rightly be given our accolades, for such has been the power of her tiny voice.'

At these words, the applause and cheering rose to a crescendo and lasted many, many minutes.

It was fortunate indeed that the shadows of the afternoon sun loomed long in the courtyard of the abbey, for the assembled villagers could not see the colour rouge that had brightened the face of the young acolyte.

... and we return to the pond:

True to her word, Monique did manage to go away for a holiday. The two-week break allowed her the time and space to rejuvenate her tired body and more importantly, to replenish her stocks of energy, which had been sorely depleted over the past months. But she did go back to the pond, and immediately upon her return resumed her duties as the director of the library.

The first day back in her office was something akin to going 'back to the future' for the date had changed, but the tasks, meetings, calls and emails were all pretty much the same as they had been before. It should be noted that the first task undertaken by Monique was to acknowledge the fine work that had been carried out by her second-in-charge and her support team of administrators and librarians – the library really had been run quite efficiently in her absence.

It was odd though, for during the course of the day, and more particularly at its end, Monique found that she was strangely ill at ease with herself. She noticed an empty feeling at the base of her stomach – certainly more of an intuitive feeling than a physiological one, but it was there nonetheless.

After she left the library in the early evening, she returned home in a kind of daze. It was not so much that her mind was unclear, it was more to do with, well, 'What now?'

It came as no surprise, as she approached the entrance to her abode, that she should find sitting on the porch, whittling away at some abstract piece of wood, none other than her friend and mentor, Gabriel.

'I truly do not know whether to kiss you or hit you,' she said with some mirth as she opened the front door.

'What do you want to hit me for?' asked Gabriel gallantly.

'Well, I've just spent the past two months going through the most horrendous of trials, and you manage to turn up when its all over. Your timing is exquisite!' she exclaimed.

'Well,' replied Gabriel, 'you didn't need me then, but it appears that you do now.'

At these words, she gave him a lasting hug and a peck on the cheek, and then set about making them both some dinner to satisfy their hunger.

The meal was conducted pretty much over a one-way conversation, for as Monique related all that had happened over the previous months, Gabriel sat for the most part listening, while diligently watching the range of emotions that crossed his friend's face.

The dishes had been done and they both retired to the living room, after-dinner drinks in hand, to sit by the fire and watch the firelight play upon the inner surfaces of the room.

Silence pervaded for a time, but then Monique said, '... and what am I supposed to do now? I feel like I've scaled Mount Everest and returned to find my home all but unchanged. But I've changed. I'm a completely different duck to the one you knew a few months ago.'

Gabriel pondered for a while and then said, 'Can I tell you a story?'

'Even if I say no, I'm sure you're going to anyway,' replied Monique.

'Well, this is the story of a mouse - born from a litter of nine, and the smallest of all the litter. One fine day the mouse's parents made plans to take all of the litter to the rubbish dump to forage for food and scraps, as was their habit. But to the little one they said, 'You have to stay home and mind the house. You're too small to help in the field, anyway.'

As you can imagine, the little fellow was crestfallen and not a wee bit angry at being left behind. So, after all the others had left, he packed a small sack of provisions and decided to go off on his own explorations. 'They're not going to leave me behind. I'll show them that I can find my own adventures.' So off he trotted, at once excited to be out on his own, but at the same time a little scared, not knowing exactly what troubles might lie in wait for him.

Our young and intrepid explorer had spent about thirty minutes wandering around the alleys and laneways adjacent to his home, when suddenly he found himself at the end of a cul de sac. All of an instant, a large grey feline jumped down from a ledge just above his eye-line.

'I love this cul de sac,' the cat mused. 'It has such a way of providing me with a whole range of sustenance.' Whereupon he calmly approached our now petrified young adventurer and promptly placed a paw on the mouse's tail to stop him from running away.

'Hmm, should have brought some salt,' said the cat, as he salivated over the top of the mouse's head.

'Stop, don't eat me,' was the plaintive cry from the besieged mouse.

'And why not?' said the amused feline.

'Well, for one, I am so scrawny and small. I would hardly make a meal for a strong and robust cat like you.'

'That doesn't concern me at all, young mouse,' and he promptly put the mouse in his mouth, swallowed, then let out a contented burp.

Then, to no one in particular, he said, 'You were always only going to be an entrée anyway.'

'Is that it – is that your story?' exclaimed an astonished Monique. 'I thought all of your stories had a happy ending?'

'Not at all. Who said that life was fair and always peachy?' replied Gabriel. 'Anyway, if a person is so stupid as to go completely outside of their capabilities, without direction, into areas that are completely unknown, then I suspect they deserve all they are going to get.'

At this, Monique threw a cushion at her friend's head and they both rolled about in laughter until tears clouded their eyes.

A pirate's model:

The interesting thing about relationships is that, for the vast majority of us, they contain a major source of the conflict, agitation, anger and annoyance we find within our daily lives. Mind you, they also contain the sweet elixir of love, companionship and sharing that betokens a king's ransom of enjoyable experiences.

Effective and open communication and a healthy dose of respect for one another are the cornerstones of a highly pleasurable relationship with a life partner, a child, sibling or parent. Yet, it is certain that each relationship will contain moments of agitation and differences of opinion.

Poland (2008) depicts a model of effective communication in the following diagram. I like to call it the "pirate model", by virtue of the R's that it contains.

The Model "SIX R's"

(Un)Reserved acceptance ________ (e.g. no scoreboard)
Request ______________________ (e.g. toilet seat)
Reaction _____________________ (e.g. land mines)

Stop here

R Repress
R Resentment
R Rejection

The portion of this model above the line indicates that we should enter into discussions with our partner/child/parent with *unreserved acceptance*. This suggests it is important not to keep a tally (or a scoreboard) of things that they have done in the past. Rather, we should treat each issue at hand without any reference to previous misdemeanours, mal-events or previously unresolved matters.

The *request* is the 'Can you?' request that we get a thousand times a day. Can you take out the garbage? Can you remove your dirty shoes before walking on the carpet? Can you make your bed? For God's sake, can you put the toilet seat down?' Mind you, these examples only relate to the home environment. Try adding in the workplace and all of its demands, such as, "Can you get this done by tomorrow?"

The *reaction* is our considered response to the request that has been received ... it's called a 'landmine'. For example, 'I am sick of you telling me to put the toilet seat down. If I want to leave it up, I'll leave it up. You put it down.' ... and so it goes.

These sorts of interactions and conflicts are quite common, are they not?

The key to this "pirate" model of communication, however, is that *it is important* to ensure that our conflicts remain *above the line,* principally because if they do not, they will produce the factors below the line.

If we walk away from an issue with it unresolved, it can turn into *repression*. Then, too much repressed and unresolved emotion can manifest as *resentment.* Excessive amounts of resentment can then turn into *rejection,* i.e. a complete breakdown in the relationship, including separation*.

*Footnote: I must tell you that a (family lawyer) client of mine said to me, after I had explained this model to her, "You have forgotten one 'R' at the end."

"What's that?" l said.

' ... Revenge,' she replied.

Conflict, as we all know, is very normal, but generally not natural, and certainly not comfortable. When, therefore, we are confronted with an issue or problem in a relationship, with a loved one, and particularly with a child, the most positive question we can ask ourselves is, "What would love do next?"

This question will catapult our thinking and feelings into a deep consideration, through the prism of love and respect for the other. It will also hasten the removal of any anger or malice that could arise when we are 'fired up'.

... let's go back to the pond:

'Gabriel,' she said, 'this is all well and good, as she wiped the tears from her eyes, 'but we haven't got to the crux of my problem. What next for me now?'

'Hmm,' he mused. 'I tell you what I'm going to do. I'm going to go out on the porch and continue my job of whittling my piece of wood. You ... you will go into your study and get a pad of paper and a pen ... off you go, go on.'

When she had duly returned with pad and pen in hand, he said, 'Now, I want you to sit down and write on the top of the first page the question: What is my heart's desire?'

As Monique obediently met his request, Gabriel continued, 'Now I want you to just sit down and write whatever comes to your mind. Don't analyse, consider or reflect – just write. Me, I'm going to sit on the porch.' And with that he strolled outside again to resume his whittling.

After half an hour or so, Gabriel came back into the room and said, with hand outstretched, 'Show me what you have written.'

'Do I have to? I mean I haven't written much, you know, and it's kind of embarrassing.'

Gabriel merely kept his hand outstretched for the paper. What he read produced a joyful smile on his face, and he said, 'It's about time.'

What was written on the paper was the simple sentence:

"I want to fall in love."

Chapter 12

You are free to be and choose as you will.

A Story: Life Choices

A young village boy was wandering aimlessly through the stalls and vendor outlets of his local marketplace. He had no coin with which to purchase goods, and his parents had shuffled him out of the house with the words, 'Go and amuse yourself; get out of the house. If you don't, you'll be given chores to do.' So rather than accept the drudgery of household chores he decided to seek amusement in the village marketplace.

As he was strolling along, a little bored, but amused nonetheless by some of the antics of the stallholders trying to attract customers, he chanced upon a few of his old mates from school. He joined them, even though they had been known troublemakers in their time at school. Despite this, he entered into their banter and responded to the playful urgings of the group.

'Hey man, what are you doin' with yourself these days?' said the first of the group.

'Ahh you know, just hangin' out, doing school stuff. You know what it's like.'

'Yeah, I remember, that stuff was a real drag you know and totally uncool. Me and the guys have been having much more fun since we left that crummy joint.'

'Yeah, what have you guys been doin?'

'Well we've kind of got a bit of a gang going. We get up to all crazy kind of stuff.'

'Yeah, like what?'

'Well, you know, this is our turf here in the village, and we just make sure that people do what we tell 'em, and make sure they pay their dues for the protection they get from us. You know what I mean?'

'Sounds kind of cool, but don't you, like, get into trouble with the police and stuff? And what about those other gangs I've heard about? Don't they give you a hard time?'

'Man, nobody messes with us. If they do, we cut them and make 'em pay.'

'Sounds pretty dangerous if you ask me.'

'Man, what are you? Some kind of pussy? Why don't you come and check it out? It's great! We just hang out and have a great time.'

Version 1:

'Well thanks anyway, but I think I'll head off home. I'll catch you guys later.'

At these words, there came a barrage of derision and poisoned invective from the gang members.

'Yeah, go on, run off home to mummy. Go and do your school work, you pussy. Next time you better get permission from your mummy to leave the house.'

These words were quite hurtful to our young fellow. But "No matter", he thought. Better to take a little verbal abuse now, than get caught up with those no-hopers. So, even though he felt somewhat chastened, he made his way back home. As he walked in the door of his home, his mother said, 'How did you go, what did you get up to?'

'Ahh nothing much, just met up with some old friends from school,' was the teenager's reply as he went to the refrigerator to make himself a snack.

Version 2:

'Yeah, well okay, it sounds kind of cool, let's go.'

So they all meandered off to the gang's hangout.

'Hey man, why don't you try some of this stuff?' said one of the guys as he took a deep drag on the reefer he had in his hand.

'What is it?'

'Oh, it's just the best shit this side of the railway line. It will relax you, don't worry.'

The young man then took a long drawback of the offered drug and immediately began to cough and splutter, much to the mirth of the assembled others.

'Do it again, it'll be better the next time', was the profound advice … and so he did.

It was only after some hours of this folly that the young man went home, with a promise to return and join them again the next day.

When he walked in the front door of his home, his mother said, 'And where in goodness have you been, I've been worried sick? What have you been doing all of this time?'

'Nothing,' retorted the young man, 'why don't you just leave me alone?' and he went into his room and slammed the door.

The concept of free will:

It must be really hard for teenagers, you know! I mean, life is challenging enough for us adults, who have fully developed brains. But according to *The Teenage Brain* web site (May 2011) "It (the teenage brain) is definitely a work in progress." This same source goes on to say:

> The greatest changes to the parts of the brain that are responsible for impulse-control, judgement, decision-making, planning, organisation and involved in other functions like emotion, occur in adolescence. This area of the brain (prefrontal cortex) does not reach full maturity until around age twenty five!

Looking back over my own history through those tumultuous years, I think it is a wonder I survived, quite frankly. My own three children are now into their teens and I begin to wonder what interesting experiences lie in wait for them, and how I, their father, may guide them through the maelstrom of challenges and experiences they will undergo in the years to come.

My goodness, with a brain still in the process of development, having to make rational judgements and sound decisions, as well as regulate one's emotions does seem a tad unfair in the scheme of things. No wonder I made so many mistakes when I was a teenager! This lack of maturity combined with full access to the liberal choices offered in our society really does make life interesting for us when we are in our teens. We hear a lot about 'free will' and this further complicates the issue.

Indeed, the concept of free will is an interesting one, and one that we should explore further. According to Walsch (1998):

> You do not have to do anything. Not in this lifetime, not in any other. You will have choice – always you will have free choice – to go anywhere you wish to go, do anything you wish to do, in your re-creation of your experience of God.

That's interesting! This sounds like an invitation to 'party hard'. It appears to offer an opportunity to 'leave it over till next time, and do it then'. But is Walsch's advice really so permissive?

If at every moment of our life's journey, we are 'defined by our actions' (see Chapter Six), and if 'What we cause to effect in others is ultimately experienced by the self' (see Chapter Nine), then the concept of 'free will' has enormous after-effects. If our choices in life are not bringing us the fulfilment we desperately seek, then, of course, we are free to change them. This is easy to say, but harder to do!

The concept of 'free will' has been debated by philosophers and scholars for millennia and the debate continues to rage, with its application to religious omnipotence and freedom of action. For example, try this definition, taken from The Stanford Encyclopaedia of Philosophy, (accessed 10.5.11):

'"Free Will" is a philosophical term of art for a particular sort of capacity of rational agents to choose a course of action from among various alternatives.'

Wow! That really messes with your head doesn't it!

Maybe, just to cater for my simple mind, we should simplify the discussion into a more palatable form, such as:

"All actions have a consequence."

For instance, I walk up to a customer service person in the local supermarket and, because I do not like the level of service she provided - I punch her in the nose.

Well, you can imagine the uproar. I would be arrested, summarily charged with assault, and given a conviction that would stain my reputation for years afterwards. These would be the consequences of my actions.

If I 'go out on the town' one evening and significantly overdo my consumption of alcohol, I can expect to have a monumental headache the next morning and a queasy feeling in my stomach. Moreover, it is unlikely that I will be able to remember what I did the night before. These will be the consequences of my actions.

So, whether or not I am free to conduct myself in whatever manner I choose (applying the concept of 'free will'), I know that whatever actions I take will have consequences. These consequences, as elaborated in Chapter Nine, will have an effect on me, and on others. If I go and punch the customer service attendant and consequently get put in prison, I am pretty sure that I will rue the stupidity of my actions. I am also sure that my mother will be saddened by the event, and my children will lose respect for their father — all these things will be the consequences of my actions.

Importantly, the tenet that "all actions have consequences" cannot be randomly or arbitrarily applied. It cannot be applied to one action and not another. We can, however, expect that the consequences will vary in their magnitude and their effect upon ourselves, as well as others.

Let's go back to the pond:

Monique awoke refreshed in the morning, and as she got out of bed, she stretched her wings to let the energy flow into her extremities. As she meandered out into the living room, she found that Gabriel had neatly packed all of his bed linen into a corner and had left a note for her on the coffee table. It read:

Dear Monique,
In life, we are free to be and to choose as we will. This is an undeniable gift from the God that gave all creatures life. Yet, with this freedom comes great responsibility, for the gift of life is a gift beyond all appreciation. It is our opportunity to experience who we really are – to know ourselves as one with the creator of all things. Should this opportunity be wasted? Can we afford to squander such a gift of grace? Is it wise to waste this gift on recklessness, indifference, or misdeeds that demonstrably cause detriment to our fellow ducks?

If we consider that every moment in life is a moment in which we can fulfil our highest potential, then we become enabled to realise the greatest worth of each moment. This does not mean that we have to build great monuments, or scale great heights, nor solve the world's problems. It can be as simple as holding the hand of your child, or kissing the cheek of your elderly grandfather as he sleeps in his chair.

Mostly though, our most defining moments can be found through love, for love is the basis of all things. Not, however, just the love for another - a child, a parent, a partner or a sibling, but more the love for oneself.

The law of attraction states, 'What you give, you receive in return'. This is the great enabler.

Seek therefore to love yourself, and express this love through all of your actions. Let your actions reflect your highest good and greatest potential, for this will in turn manifest the love of others in your life.

I will see you when next your spirit calls – it will be the last time you have to call.

Yours,

Gabriel

A Story: Droplets, Ripples and Waves

The master and novice were strolling down one of the many pathways that surrounded their abbey. These pathways were many and each one provided a unique aspect of the divine nature of the abbey's existence. Some pathways meandered through the lush garden. Others wound through deep forest, whilst another had a waterfall at its destination. The particular pathway that both master and novice traversed this day ended at a beautiful pond surrounded by a vivid array of the most divine native flowers in bloom.

The conversation between the two devotees this day had been a propos of nothing much at all. They spoke about the weather and the beauty of their surroundings. As they approached the pond, the young novice casually picked up a pebble and threw it into the calm, still water. The resulting ripples were gentle and serene but numerous, defying the novice's efforts to count them on their way to the bank of the pond. The master then said to the young man, 'Go over and pick up that large rock by the side of the pond and cast it into the water.'

Without questioning his master, the young novice bent down to pick up the rather large rock and then cast it with all his might into the water. The resultant splash was extremely large. So much so, that both master and novice were splashed by the many droplets that flew into the air.

'Could you count the ripples on that occasion?' asked the master of his novice.

'No master, I could not. The ripples were again too numerous to count.'

'Yes, this is quite so,' replied the master, 'but what has

happened to the pond now?'

'Master, the pond has returned to the normal calm state it held previously.'

'My young novice, this is how it appears on the surface, but in reality the nature of the pond has been changed forever.'

'Master, I do not understand.'

'What you see on the surface of the pond appears to be the same, but under the surface the pond has been forever altered. The pond now contains one small pebble and one large rock that will be with it forever. The nature of the pond has been forever changed as a consequence of your throwing in these two rocks. It will never forget the day that you cast the two rocks into its depths.'

'Master, I know that you are trying to teach me something with this example, but I am afraid that my mind just does not grasp the truth of it.'

'My young novice, the pond is like our true self — our soul or true nature, if you prefer. The pebble and rock represent our actions in life. Sometimes we take actions that have very minor consequences. Others, like the big rock, have consequences that are grave and disturbing. Our true nature is forever changed as a consequence of the actions that have been taken. The ripples of the pond, which were too many to count, represent what we have effected in others, by virtue of our actions. They are impossible to count, but they have been numerous even so.'

'I say to you therefore, before you cast a rock into your pond, before you take some action in your life, give pause to consider the consequences that your actions will have, not just for yourself, but for the many others in your life who will endure their lingering affects.'

... we return to the pond:

Monique couldn't help but smile at the letter left by her dear friend. She had come to understand the depth of wisdom in every one of Gabriel's actions and words. Nothing was superfluous or mundane. To him, each moment was important and she had come to realise how much she treasured the times that they spent together.

With these thoughts dancing in her head, she made her way into the library to commence the days' work, greeting staff members as she traversed the corridors leading to her office.

Around midday, when she finally emerged from the barrage of phone calls and emails, she decided to take a walk through the hallowed halls of the library and go directly to the room that, now once more, contained the sacred *Book of Mysteries.* A quaint smile flitted across her face as she entered the room and saw the book standing proudly, in its rightful place, in the centre of the room.

Of a sudden, and completely on a whim, she decided to switch off the alarm and upgraded security system that had been installed to secure the book's wellbeing, and she picked up the book. Just to make sure it was real and to feel the weight and presence of the treasured manuscript. As she did so the pages flew open, as if some great wind had captured the thin pages and cast them asunder. It startled her so much that she almost dropped the tome onto the floor.

Gingerly, she placed the book back on the stand and randomly opened the pages to wherever the fates dictated. As she did so, one of the pages fluttered to the floor. She was aghast. 'What have I done?' she said to herself, as the colour blanched from her cheeks. 'I have ripped one of the pages. Oh, my God! What am I going to do?'

Unconsciously, she looked around to see if anybody had seen what had happened and at once felt relieved that she was on her own. As she bent down to pick up the torn page from the floor, she felt the feathers on the back of her neck rise, as if in response to the presence of some unseen spirit, there with her in the room. She noticed that the edge of the page was not jagged and torn, as it would be if it had been carelessly rendered. Rather, the edge was sliced, as if by some magical guillotine or sharp blade. Then she looked at what was written on the page. It was a letter, a letter addressed to her. It was another letter across time from her great grandfather and it read:

My dearest Monique,
I am so grateful that I have had the opportunity to become a part of your life. Even though we have never met in the flesh, we are indeed one in spirit. This is how I come to know of your grace and beauty, as well as your trials and tribulations.

Already, in your life, you have achieved many things, and what you have done for your community will have a lasting effect across many generations and lives.

Though your life has been as yet brief, you have nevertheless come to understand that the consequences of your actions are far reaching – even going past the divide you call death, though in truth, there is no such divide – everything is life.

Through your actions, you have also come to understand what you are truly capable of realising within yourself. The many trials that you have faced have brought these capabilities to the fore.

And so, you ask yourself, 'What now?' but this is not the right question. The right question is, 'What would love do next?' If it is love that you seek, do not try to find it in another. Rather, seek to realise it within yourself. When you do this, you will discover that it has never been further away than your heartbeat. Know also that 'love cannot be found', for in truth, it has never gone anywhere that you are not.

I say to you therefore, 'Love who you are and what you do. Do not fear what life may have in store for you. Rather, embrace each of the experiences that you have, for they bring you ever closer to the realisation of who you really are'. I can tell you, from where I now sit - the person you have become and are now, makes me smile a lot.

Go forth from here with love and gratitude in your heart, and the consequences of your actions will be blessed by the divine. And remember, 'You cannot hurt God, you can only do harm to yourself', for each and all of us are one in the spirit of the divine.

Go with grace. Oh, and don't feel bad about the page falling out – I designed it that way. Haha.

Your loving great grandfather

Alfred

As she read these final words, Monique burst into laughter until the tears cascaded down her cheeks and a burly security guard came to enquire what all the noise was about.

Chapter 13

If you look upon life as a gift, you will see it as a treasure that will serve you always.

A story: My Eyes Held Despair

A monk returned to the abbey unexpectedly one day, and his arrival was the cause of much celebration and rejoicing. He had been on a pilgrimage for over two years and he had been sorely missed by the other monks and the novices of the abbey. As he entered the gates, he was surrounded by old friends and well-wishers who assailed him with questions of his travels, all of them seeking tales of the world beyond the walls of the abbey.

After breaking fast and taking a well-earned bath, our monk took up his station upon a meditation mat in the main courtyard and was immediately set upon by the many who wished to hear his story. As he related tales of his travels and travails, the courtyard filled to overflowing with eager ears, and an abundance of questions, all of which the monk answered, often to the open-mouthed astonishment of the listeners. Eventually though, after many hours of story-telling and with the sun beginning its descent upon the horizon, the master of the abbey came into the courtyard and bade our travelling monk retire to the master's chambers for refreshments and further conversation.

As our monk entered into the sacred chamber of the master monk, he fell to his knees and pressed his forehead to the ground in reverence and respect.

'Rise my young traveller,' said the Master, 'and tell me tales of your journey.' And the master gestured towards the mat placed directly opposite his chair.

It was then that a sallow paleness came over the visage of our young monk, as if he had been assaulted by some bad memory or abhorrent thought.

'What ails you, young man? What is cause of your frown that replaces the wonder of your smile?' asked the master of the abbey.

'Master,' replied the young monk, 'I tell you that I am greatly pleased to be back here in the abbey, for in truth it is a safe haven from the many trials that exist beyond the sanctity of these walls.'

'Master,' he continued, 'in my two years of travelling, I have seen much that torments my spirit and disturbs my sleep. I have seen abominable acts committed against my fellow man. I have seen murder, pestilence, greed and avarice. I have seen acts of treachery and violence against the weak and poor in our society. In truth, Master, I have seen much that sorely tests my belief in the sanctity of man. I fear the absence of the divine. My eyes have beheld many things that have caused me to challenge my own faith in God. Even now, as I sit before you, I feel abject, lost, and ready to exit these walls, never to return again with the title of monk.'

The master closed his eyes for many moments after these words, but when he again opened his eyes, his gaze was full of love and compassion for the young monk who sat at his feet.

'My son,' said the master, 'that you have been witness to these many tribulations is both a gift of great magnitude and a test of your faith like no other.'

'But master, how can these things be a gift? I have seen murder, pillage and pestilence where many suffered and many died … surely this cannot be a gift?'

'My son, what you have witnessed is man's fight against his own true nature.'

'But master, I do not understand.'

'Always,' continued the master, 'man fights what he fears the most and what he fears he makes real. The poor man envies the rich man and despises him for his wealth. The rich man despises the poor man for fear that the wretch will take his possessions.

The woman screams abuse and scorn at the man she feels has wronged her, only to forget that she willingly brought him into her life to secure her future. The villager amasses great volumes of grain for fear of one day being in need, when his neighbour has nothing to eat because his crops have failed.'

'But master, what are you saying? Are you saying that man brings all his misery upon himself? That none of these trials are retribution from a judgemental God?'

'My son, I say to you that at the root of all of these trials and tribulations is man's limited definition of self.'

'Master, what do you mean?'

'It is our definition of 'self' that is our greatest limitation, and cause for much of our suffering! Would it be possible for you to murder another if you saw the other as a part of yourself? Would we dare to steal from others if we knew we were stealing from ourselves? Could we refuse starving persons something to eat, if we knew they were our brothers in spirit?'

'In truth, I say to you, my young monk, we see ourselves as separate from one another, and therein lie the origins of many of our trials and tribulations. If we were to look upon all others as kindred spirits – all one in the eyes of God – then we would not do unto others the many things that we do now. We could not, for we would know that what we do to others, we do to ourselves. Thus, at man's highest stage of evolution, if he truly loves himself, he will love all others as the self. Do you see, young monk, how far man has yet to evolve in these matters?'

'Yes master, I do see how far we are yet to evolve. I say also that I will not tarry a long time in the abbey, for this truth lies yet unrevealed to many and there is much that I have yet to do to realise it outside of these walls.'

'Go with God now, my young son and know that there will never be an absence of love in anything that you do.'

'Thank you master,' said the young monk.

Love is the answer – what is the question?

In Chong (2011) - as an excerpt from *The Book of Mysteries* I wrote,

> Love does not discriminate, nor does love have any bounds or limitations, but as you treasure another, so must you treasure yourself, for truly each of you is an irreplaceable child of God. The love that you would give to another, you must also bestow upon yourself. Treasure who you are and realise that the body, mind and spirit that you are is a joy beyond all knowing for the God that gave you life everlasting.

Yet, throughout the ages we have sought, and continue to seek the love of another to *make ourselves complete*, to *fill the void* or to *make us feel whole*. It is as if we continue to go through life as a *glass half full*, in search of the other who can *fill our cup*.

Indeed *to fall in love* is one of the most miraculous occurrences that will ever befall a human being. I think the experience of falling in love must feel like the elation one receives from scaling a difficult mountain or winning an Olympic gold medal. To feel love for a partner, child, parent or sibling is a gift beyond our most vivid imaginings.

How can we best describe the intensity of these feelings? Do these words or phrases do them justice?

- Ecstasy;
- Happiness;
- Pure bliss;
- Elation;
- Delight;
- Profound pleasure.

These feelings, when applied to love, represent some of the most intense feelings that we can ever experience in life. But, is this all there is? Does it take another for us to *fill our cup*, to ensure that we experience these wonders?

I wrote in the *Book of Testaments* (2009),

"According to the *Oxford Reference Dictionary* (1995), to know is to, 'have in mind; have learned; be able to recall'."

Yet in the context of our awareness, is that all that knowing is? To *know* something is quite different from the *experience* of something, which is quite different from the *feeling* of something.

I used as an example of this distinction, the experience of riding a super-fast motorbike around a speedway. I could say that I *know* how to ride a super-bike. But this would be quite different from the *experience* of riding the super-bike around the track. Which is quite different again from the *feeling* I would get from riding the super-bike around the track.

So, we see from this example, that *knowing* something only gives us partial awareness. The *experience* also only provides a partial awareness of the depth of the experience. But adding what we *feel* gives us a complete and total awareness and understanding of the experience we are having.

... meanwhile back at the pond (some six months later);

Monique was sitting by the small waterfall at the southern end of the pond. It was a place that she had more frequently come to over the past months. It was a comfortable place in which she could share her thoughts and feelings with the sound of the water as it cascaded over the falls. It was an elixir to her spirit and a welcome respite from the constant eager activity of the library's business bustle. She would often bring her favourite book to read, or her scribble pad on which she would jot her thoughts and dreams. Some of these she kept, others she would discard as too fanciful, or not within the realms of possibility.

At these times, she also enjoyed the squeals of the children at play as they cavorted through and about the falls. She would often wonder what it would be like to have a gabble of young ducklings in and under her wing. She didn't feel any sense of lack from these thoughts; rather, as a realist, she knew that 'there had to be a horse before the cart', in that she had to find a partner before she could contemplate the prospect of children. Of course, from her readings, she was aware of the new technology available in the world of ducks, that would allow the prospect of motherhood without the physical presence of a drake. Perhaps, she mused, it was just her old-fashioned family values that helped her dismiss this train of thought.

It was late afternoon at the pond and she noticed that a fine mist or fog had descended and cast an almost surreal presence upon the water. The phenomenon was highly unusual at this time of year. She looked up from the book she had been reading and noticed a young couple swimming by the waterfall. They were obviously rapturously in love and could barely restrain their affections, despite their being in a public place. They looked into each other's eyes deeply, each touched the other's cheek and they gently caressed each other's plumage. At the same time she saw another couple, whose plumage had turned to grey. They were swimming contentedly together, side-by-side, each comfortable in the presence of the other. They were not sharing words or deep affection, merely enjoying each other's presence, as they contemplated the waterfall.

The fact that these two couples were there, content with each other's company, caused Monique to feel joy in the delight of other people's happiness, but also something else that she had, it seems, repressed for some time. She felt lonely. That was interesting, she thought; she was alone, but that was generally not a problem, as she enjoyed her own company. Yet, never before in her life had she experienced the empty feeling of being lonely. The feeling was new to her ... and it was quite profound.

'What is this?' she said to no one in particular. 'This is not like me?'

But rather than dismiss the feeling out of hand, she acknowledged its presence and said a quiet thank you for its revelation.

She decided she would wait for any further manifestation of it in her life ... and the manifestation arrived within days. Over the next two months, the feeling of loneliness began to grow and grow, until it seemed to engulf her in a paroxysm of overwhelming emotion. Sure, she continued to work hard, and to all observers she maintained her regal demeanour and outward calm. But inside, she felt abjectly lonely.

In all this time, she continued to attend numerous functions, and meet dignitaries and other people from all stations and cultures. She met some wonderful people, yet at the end of it all, there was still something missing.

A story: I Missed my Mother

All was quiet as the attending monk walked past the dormitory of the young first-year novices. He made his way to the end of the corridor and was about to turn around and make his way back, when he heard a faint sniffle. His ears now pricked in attentiveness, he stopped walking and listened for the origin of the sound. He heard it again, and this time he identified it. One of the young novices was crying.

As he walked down the passageway separating the rows of beds, each containing a sleeping form, he saw the sharp rise and fall of the bedding, identifying the lad who was weeping.

The monk gently beckoned the lad to rise and come with him into the lounge area of the dormitory where they could talk and uncover the cause of the lad's distress.

'What ails you my friend?' said the monk with empathy for the distressed novice.

At this question, the boy once again collapsed into an avalanche of tears and anguish. The monk merely handed the young novice a tissue to dry his eyes and waited patiently while the tears abated.

Soon enough, the tears slowed and the novice's heaving chest returned to normal. Then, once again, the monk gently enquired as to the source of the trouble.

'I miss my mother. I want to go home,' was the plaintive cry from the young minion.

The monk at once felt great compassion for the young novice, and then said, 'Can I tell you a true story?'

'Yes,' came the whispered reply.

'Well, when I was your age I went on a school excursion. It was a three-day journey with a whole lot of other children in the company of a few teachers from my school. Well, you know, I had a terrible time. I missed my mother so badly. I was so sad, and I cried every night into my pillow so that the other children would not hear me.'

'Is that true?' asked the novice. 'Did you really cry yourself to sleep?'

'Yes I did.'

'And what happened then?'

'Well, when we returned to school, each of us who had been on the excursion had to stand before the class and tell everyone what they enjoyed about the camp.'

'And what did you say to the class?'

'Well, you know, all of the other children said that they really enjoyed the camp, had a lot of fun and made a lot of friends. But when it was my turn to speak, I told them that I really hated the camp. Then, the teacher said, "You missed your mother didn't you?"'

'Yes,' I replied in a whisper. Then some of the students started to say nasty things like, 'mummy's boy' and 'what a sissy'. I felt pretty bad, I can tell you.'

'And what happened then?'

'Well nothing really, except that I recall this event as really important and quite distressing when I was young. But now that I am older, I see that I was mistaken.'

'But master, how were you mistaken?'

'Well now, I am able to see that my tears were fashioned

through a cauldron of love, the love I felt, and still feel, for my mother. For me now, those tears I shed so many years ago have been the foundation of the love and respect I have for my mother. A greater blessing a man could never have.'

'So, young man,' continued the monk, 'do not let your tears be a cause for sorrow; rather know that each tear represents a jewel of love that will bind you to your mother's heart from here till the end of days. Now go back to bed and sleep soundly until the morning brings renewal to the earth.'

... back at the pond:

Monique had returned to the waterfall one afternoon, and much to her surprise there was no one else around. To be sure, the weather had turned a little chilly and the wind ruffled the edges of the cape that shielded her from the cool breeze. The waterfall itself continued its cascade, completely indifferent to the thoughts and trials of those that graced its presence and enjoyed its benevolence.

Monique bent down to pick up a small pebble, and casually tossed it into the water to watch the gentle ripples meander to the bank of the pond. Then, all of a sudden, she began to cry ... in great sobs of anguish that made her chest heave without cease. Her tears flowed, almost in concert with the waterfall.

Then, from a distance, she heard the words, as if as an echo had bounced from the channels that surrounded the pond,

'I told you this would be the last time you had to call.'

But she could not make out where the voice was coming from, although it did have a familiar cadence to it.

'Who is this? What is your name? What do you want?' asked Monique of the disembodied voice.

'Didn't you ask me these same questions, the first time we met?'

The answer came from directly behind her. She swung around to see who had spoken. It was Gabriel! And the look of relief, excitement and bewilderment in Monique's eyes, could only be matched by the love that shone in his own.

Without words, they embraced as if time stood still, as only people in love can honestly do.

After many moments in silence, Gabriel said, 'Do you know that I have been waiting for you all this time?'

'I'm so glad you have,' replied Monique.

The lovers then embraced once more, this time with unrestrained passion.

Chapter 14

Love, caress and care for things, but remember you do not own them.

… we remain at the pond:

The evening passed in ecstasy, passion and release for the two who now became one. It was a passion born of the enlightenment of two hearts entwined, and it was a release from previous bondages of mind, caught in the grip of loneliness and need. As the minutes turned into hours, they fell asleep in each other's arms. The fire extinguished itself in the early hours of the chilly new day.

In the morning, as she rubbed the sleep from her eyes, Monique could immediately smell the pungent aroma of the freshly brewed coffee and she could hear the sizzle of some delicacy in the process of preparation.

'Good morning beautiful being,' was Gabriel's greeting as he busied himself in the kitchen.

Monique simply sidled up to him with the grace of a cat and embraced him with a passion that seemed to show no abatement, despite the lasting nature of the previous evening's exertions.

'Peace, woman! Even the most able-bodied amongst us need to recover their energies in preparation for future engagements,' said Gabriel with a laugh. 'I have prepared for you a feast befitting a queen and if you continue to stir my passions, I'll burn the eggs from distraction.'

They delighted in each other's company over what was a repast spent mostly in silence, until the last mouthful was taken.

'Do you know,' said Monique, 'apart from you being the nephew of my father's old mentor, Mandrake. I actually know nothing about you.' You just turn up in my life, when I seem to need you the most. Then you up and disappear without word or trace, until the next time I dissolve into some miasma of distress or ill fortune.'

'Only partly true, my dear one. You don't know what I do, but you do know the contents of my heart. Otherwise I would not be here with you now.'

'Hmm, your heart is as pure as the winter snow, of this I am sure, but you cannot eat the contents of your heart, nor can you live in the warmth of its glow. There must be something that you do, and somewhere that you go?'

'My love, ever the practical one, I see. Well let me tell you this. I have rejuvenated the old home of Mandrake, which grew to need much repair as he ventured into old age and suffered a limited capacity for work. I must also express much gratitude for his benevolence, for in addition to the legacy of spiritual awareness that he passed on through his genes, he left me a small monetary legacy that provides for my financial stability and wellbeing.'

'But how do you pass the hours of your days?' asked Monique with a quizzical look. 'I can barely find time in any day to scratch an itch under my eider, let alone contemplate the nature of the universe.'

'Well, that obviously explains why I have waited so long for your loving embrace. I knew in my soul the first moment we met that I loved you with all of my heart.'

'Do you mean to say that you have been waiting for me all of this time, while I was too busy to realise what was truly in my heart?'

'Yep!' came the prompt reply.

'Well why didn't you say something? I mean, you could have given me some sign, some indication of your deepest feelings. Perhaps even a hint of intention or purpose.'

'Hmm, perhaps! But it is like when you hear a sound through a dense fog. You don't know from where the sound is coming, or how far away is the source. I merely waited for the fog to lift and the sun to shine through, before I made the call.'

'And what now, my dearest Gabriel, where do we go from here?'

'Ahh, just like a woman to ponder upon questions of depth and magnitude when more pressing matters present themselves as an opportunity,' he said as he embraced Monique with a passion and an urgency that was totally irresistible. And the remainder of the day was spent in that way.

Big things from little things grow:

My partner has the dolorous crying sound of her dear friend's three-month old newly born child as a recording on her mobile phone. Every time somebody rings her, the ring tone echoes the sound of this young infant's colic pain.

Interesting! For my part, I am well past the time when I would actively seek the intervention of a child's distress to attract me whenever someone phones me – but each to their own. I am absolutely sure that many of my habits and eccentricities would grate upon my partner's sensibilities. Indeed, how she puts up with them is a question that defies the wisdom of the ages.

Love is grand, is it not? So full of the greatest peaks of passion and pleasure, yet so replete with the irritations of the mundane. But the great thing about love is that it is the really little things that make big things grow ... the gentle touch on the cheek, a smile on the face and in the voice, a laugh perhaps. Each and all freely given, without expectation of return.

It is the touch that says, 'I love you'. It is the smile that says 'You are safe and everything is alright'. It is the laugh that overcomes the challenges that confront a pair on their life's journey together. Each and all given in a frequency commensurate with the needs of the day, and not just on birthdays, anniversaries, or festive occasions.

These thoughts must indeed lead us to a golden rule:

"Give a little of your love, every day."

A story: Can I Show You My Drawings?

The old man was sitting contentedly in his garden, watching the dance of the flowers and the trees as they swayed gleefully to the rhythm of the breeze. All of a sudden his grandson came bounding out of the backdoor yelling excitedly, 'Grandpa, grandpa!' whereupon he was immediately swept up in his grandfather's arms and given a loving embrace of welcome.

The two then sat contentedly together, the grandson on his grandfather's lap. After a little time, the young lad enquired, 'How come you're so old, Grandpa?'

'Well, you know my boy, the passage of time does cause the body to lose its vigour. The old bones tend to creak, and the hair turns to white. But what you don't see is the vigour and beauty in one's heart.'

'But yes I do,' came the unexpected reply.

'How so, young man?'

'Well Grandpa, I see that you are wise and have lots of love for everybody. When I speak to you, you really listen. You don't tell me things, but ask me what I think. When I show you my drawings, you really look at them and don't just say, 'Ah that's nice'.

On hearing these words, the kindly grandfather nearly burst with pride for his young grandson.

'And how much, young man, do you value these things?'

'Grandpa, they mean more to me than anything else in the whole world.'

The old man looked lovingly at his offspring and said, 'And these things are so freely given aren't they? Perhaps we should give them more often, what do you say? ... let's go and play a game.'

'Yehhh!' was the reply as the boy jumped from his grandfather's lap in search of the ball.

… let's return to the pond (three months later):

Monique returned from her work at the library this evening to find that Gabriel had prepared a wonderful array of dishes fit for a king.

'Not only are you a gentle spirit, my dear Gabriel, you are also useful to have around the house,' said Monique as she entered the door and placed a kiss upon his upturned cheek.

'Might I be permitted to stay around for a few more days then?' said Gabriel in retort.

'Mmph, how about forever, would that be okay?'

'My dear lady, forever has the connotation of a promise that is impossible to keep. I can no more promise you forever, than I can give you the moon and the sun. But what I can give you is the totality of who I am in each and every moment we have together.'

'Ahh, you drakes, always on the look out for a pathway to avoid commitment! Why is it so hard for you to settle down with one woman? To say I will love you forever and cast aside the need to sow your wild oats?'

'My dearest, you ask me to promise a future which I can neither control nor even predict. Yet, in my heart I know that our being together is, and always will be, for a divine purpose.'

'And what do you think is that purpose?' asked Monique.

'Our union, divine in my eyes, is for us both to realise who we truly are. It is to remember our true oneness with the creator of all things. This we will do as one, each for the other. In truth, our union will be eternal in love as we are bound by the solemnity of purpose, rather than the bondage of promise.'

'You know Gabriel, you should write a book.'

'If I were to write a book, it would be a book about love, and you would be the central character, for my heart is eternally yours.'

'You know,' said Monique, 'given that you spend most of your time here anyway, why don't you just move in and we can live our divine purpose under the one roof.'

'As always you are the practical one. Anyway, it seems that our union is public knowledge anyway,' he said, as he handed Monique a copy of the latest gossip magazine published in the pond district.

The headline on page two from the *News of the Pond* read, 'Director of the Library in a Love Match of her Own' and the picture showed both Monique and Gabriel sharing a kiss by the waterfall.

'Aren't some of these reporters eminently resourceful?' quipped Monique.

'Well it's lucky that I have a mind to be with you forever,' said Gabriel. 'At least in this way we might contain their enthusiasm, and avoid the boredom of the same pictures appearing over and again in the years to come.'

'Hmmm, I hope they don't photograph me first thing in the morning,' said Monique, 'I'd hate to be caught with my plumes out of place.'

They both looked at one another and laughed till their sides hurt.

Purpose, not possession:

My very dear friend, Chris Shaw, provided some very sage advice to us mere males in his wonderful book, *How To Get More Nookie* (2012). He said that there are two principal elements to an enduring love-match between consenting adults. The first is "respect". He included, as a subset to this critical element, the following set of crucial ingredients:

- Don't Take Your Partner For Granted;
- Watch Your Table Manners;
- Don't Put Your Partner Down, ever;
- Maintain Cleanliness;
- (No) Belching And Farting, and

- Don't Forget the Foreplay.

The second principal element is "communication" and under this rather broad umbrella, Chris has suggested:

- Listening;
- Friendship;
- Consultation;
- Maturity;
- Trustworthiness, and
- Responsibility.

Now, each of these topics would merit a chapter on its own, but I will leave you to define what each of these categories means for you. Either that, or you could read Chris's book for an explanation and description far beyond my capacity to relate. However, I will speak with you about how you can be 'purposeful' in each of these areas.

The fundamental tenet of being 'purposeful' in the critical area of 'our relationships' has been described in *The Music of the Soul,* Chong (2011) as one of the three great pillars of our life. The other two are identified as 'our health' and 'money'. The presence of unhappy or tumultuous relationships in our life is cause for considerable distress and anguish. It is cause for much anxiety, worry and stress and will have a deleterious impact on other areas of our life, such as our career, finances or peace of mind.

For me, being 'purposeful' means that these areas of my life are critically important and therefore deserve the best of my attention and the extent of my capacity to endeavour to realise the fullness of relationship. This *attention* means that I need to devote time and effort to their betterment and improvement. It means I should not take the relationship for granted nor assume that everything will work out as I would wish. It will take time and effort for these important things to happen.

For me, it also means that I have no ownership of the other person. It is a quaint and restrictive figure of speech that says, 'This is *my* spouse or partner. This is *my* child or *my* mother or father.' I do not own them. They are not a possession, like a car, or a house. How is it possible to *own* another person? To place such a limitation on another would restrict their capacity to be free to feel, live and experience themselves as who they really are.

In terms of my relationship with my partner, whom I love dearly, the crux of the matter is that our being together is divine beyond imagining, but the analogy I would draw for it is that of the bird living in a golden cage – with the door always open. It is the expression of love through respect, open communication and trustworthiness that induces the other to stay, not any ownership of the other, nor the promise of eternal love. It is the commitment to purposefully engage and enhance our respect for each other and to communicate openly that will give wings to its grandeur.

A story: Not a Day Goes By

An elderly couple were sitting on a park bench. The old man was feeding the pigeons with handfuls of bread he had brought along for the cause. His wife of many years was by his side, knitting a sweater for her grandchild, and the clickety-clack of the needles made a constant accompaniment to the sound of the birds as they chirped merrily going about their labours.

Most of the time was spent in silence, both partners replete with love and full of contentment. Then, all of sudden, a ball came flying across the park after an errant kick from one of the children at play. The ball came rolling towards the old couple, scattering the pigeons, and managed to roll under their feet.

'Can I have my ball back please mister?' came the earnest plea from the young child who had kicked the ball.

'Sure, son,' said the old man as he bent down to pick up the ball.

'Here,' said the old man as he hurled it with all his might back to the young lad.

'Thank you,' the boy replied.

'You're welcome,' said the old man.

Then after a minute or two, the old lady said to her husband, 'You know dear, that experience with the child's ball reminds me of our relationship together over all of these years.'

The old man looked at his wife with a quizzical expression on his face. 'What on earth do you mean, dear?' said the old man.

'Well, you know, over the many years of our union, we have dealt with a few curve balls in our life, haven't we dear?'

'We certainly have!'

'And we've managed to work through them together, by talking things through and working with one another, haven't we dear?'

'We certainly have!'

'We've also managed to treat ourselves and others with respect and kindness, just like you did with the young child, haven't we dear?'

'Yes, we certainly have.'

'Over the years, we've managed to provide for our family and share what we've got with others, don't you think dear?'

'Yes, my love, but do you think these are the reasons why we've stayed together all of these years?' asked the man of his wife.

'Oh yes, these are some of the reasons, but not the main one.'

'Huh? Not the main one! Are there other things more important than these?'

'Well, you know dear,' said the old lady, 'there has not been a day gone by, in all of the years we have been together, that I have not said, 'Thank God you are here.''

The old man merely smiled and planted a kiss upon his wife's wrinkled cheek.

Chapter 15

Whatever you wish to create for yourself, create for another.

… let us return to the pond:

On this day Monique's and Gabriel's attention was attuned to the most recent meeting of the 'Council of Elders', those elected members of the community charged with managing and governing the pond's daily affairs and legal processes. On the agenda was a debate over a rather large sum of money, namely the million dollars provided to the council by the recent demise of the once-powerful Master Vladimir, formerly leader of the Brotherhood of Ecumenical Light. The management and distribution of this significant amount challenged and occupied the members of the council for much of the afternoon.

For their part, both Monique and Gabriel had made a submission to council to have the money placed in trust, under strict rules of distribution. Gabriel alone was to manage the distribution of the funds from the trust and only for the benefit of the pond and its inhabitants. Here is a part of the proposal they made to the council.

"It is acknowledged that the library has brought unprecedented levels of growth and prosperity to certain sections of the pond. Yet, it is also clear that this growth has spawned social inequality and division, as well being responsible for a considerable rise in the level of crime within the pond community. This rise in the level of crime has brought an increase in the rate of incarceration, particularly among the young, our so-called juvenile offenders."

Monique highlighted the fact, and the council agreed, that this trend was not a healthy sign for the future functioning, sustainability and prosperity of the pond community, particularly over the long term.

Given the pressing need for a remedy and the availability of such a large sum of money, it was agreed that urgent action should be taken. It was also agreed that all disbursement of the funds must occur under strict guidelines of acquittal and audit. The proposal presented by Monique and Gabriel was accepted unanimously. An action plan for the future was formulated, involving Gabriel as the duck responsible for much of the work. He would also be accountable for its outcomes. Monique, for her part, would remain in her current position as Director of the Library, but she too would be charged with the added responsibility of being a trustee, along with three other members of the Council.

Released from the stuffy confines of the meeting room, both Monique and Gabriel walked outside into the cool afternoon air. They looked at one another with a mixture of relief, expectation, and anticipation. It was Gabriel who spoke first.

He said, 'You know, my love, I have noticed that when we do things, it is by no means in half measure.'

'Well, my sweet, if we are going to do something, it may as well be big, for we do not serve the world by thinking small.'

'Yes, this is true, and I hasten to add that I can neither design nor divine where this pathway takes us, but it certainly feels right. In my heart I know that this is our calling, irrespective of results or outcomes.'

'Hmm,' quipped Monique, 'perhaps we should ponder the future possibilities over a glass of our cellar's finest. I can sense an idea or two burgeoning, but it requires the quiet of our home and the warmth of a fire to give impetus to our creativity and imagination.'

'Excellent suggestion, and might I suggest take-away Chinese for dinner? I hear the noodles are superb.'

So the two made their way to the local fast-food outlet to buy dinner and then wander home. But on the way home they noticed a significant increase in the amount of graffiti on walls and fences. They also saw youths languishing in a general state of idleness, hanging around, obviously bored and in need of distraction. They also saw evidence of drug-taking from the refuse left in the corridors and by-ways. As Monique and Gabriel looked at one another, it was plain that they were thinking the same thing. The cogs of both minds were spinning with ideas and possibilities.

A Story: The Greatest Version of Your Grandest Vision

It was not often that the grand master ventured from his monastery high up in the mountains of his own country. Many were the demands upon his time and the requests for his sage utterances. His wisdom and compassion had influenced many lives and, over the years many had come to his doorstep to seek wise counsel and comfort for their tormented spirits. Although now well advanced in years, his body still remained lithe along with a mind that was acute, with an intelligence steeped in happiness and benevolence. His capacity for humour was well known amongst his many devotees.

It was with great concern for the fate of mankind that he decided to journey to far parts of the earth to spread his message of peace and goodwill, and to prepare the many for the future trials that he knew the world was about to endure.

His first port of call, paradoxically, was not made to a poor or impoverished country, but rather, to what many would consider as a wealthy, well-developed, first-world country.

Many wanted to come and listen to the grand master. They wanted to catch a glimpse of the holy man who had ventured so far from his home to speak. But again, paradoxically, the grand master chose to speak first with the leaders, politicians and eminent academics in the community, before mingling with the community members at large.

This, in part, is what he said:

'You are the leaders and great visionaries of your community. You live in a country where the basic human requirements of life are well provided for. You are a prosperous nation; the majority of your citizens are well nourished and provided with high standards of health care. Your infant mortality rates are low and your children are predominantly well educated. Yet, despite these advancements, I say to you that in comparison with many others on our planet you are misguided in much of what you do.'

At these words, there was an uncomfortable murmur amongst the assembled dignitaries, with much shuffling in the seats to signify their discomfort with the wise man's words. But he continued ...

'You have reached a stage in your progress where your continued drive towards ever more improvements in your living standards no longer serves you well as a community.'

Once again, there was a murmur amongst the assembled; one voice was even raised in protest and anger at the grand master's words. But he held his hand forth to acknowledge their disquiet, while seeking their patience to hear the remainder of his words.

'You seek strength by improving your standards of living, but remain unaware of, or are unable to deal with the consequences of your compulsion. The measure of any society should not simply be a commitment to growth and prosperity, but rather a dedication to 'matters of community'. You need to take account of matters such as these: the social democratic principles of cooperation - rather than the current adversarial nature of your politics; the opportunity of high standards of education for all; the inclusion of all minorities; and, last but not least, a commitment to equality. Your society lists to one side with the ever-expanding inequality among its diverse peoples. The gap between those that have more and those that have less is the greatest cause of your burgeoning rates of crime and increasing rates of imprisonment. Your communities show an absence of compassion for those that are marginalised and in need –

perhaps out of fear that the well-off may lose their standard of living as benefits are re-distributed to the poor.

As a society, you must interact with one another on levels well beyond those of commerce and economics. The many amongst you who are disabled have no less potential than the rest, but they remain marginalised and stigmatised. Your young people, the future of your country, are confronted with the scourges of drugs, alcohol, and gambling, overtly marketed to them through your multitudinous media channels with their hedonistic promises of fame and fortune. Then there are the mind-numbing amusements of the digital and social media. I say to you truly that you must better harness the passion and energy of your young people. If it can be re-directed to alleviating your social and community ills, you will lessen their focus upon themselves, as they seek to benefit others in their communities.'

At these words, the auditorium was completely silent. You could hear the air hissing from the vents in the ceiling. Then the grand master spoke again and said, 'I will now take your questions.'

At this invitation, one of the political leaders stood up and asked to speak.

'Grand master, if we as leaders of our community do not continue to struggle to improve our living standards, will this not mean the death-knell of our society? Not to mention the limitation of our own tenure as leaders?'

'A brave question indeed,' replied the grand master, 'but I say to you that positive change requires not that you refrain from seeking progress, but rather that you seek a realisation of untapped potential.'

'Master, I don't understand,' came the response from the questioner.

'In your society you are well past the point where increases in living standards have much bearing on the basic requirements of human life. But you are yet to realise and use the full range of potential within your own walls. I mentioned before your youth, and the disabled. But you even reject the elderly with all of their wisdom and experience. They have the time to teach the younger ones amongst you. You cast them aside into homes and villages away from the comforts of family, and the needs of your younger children. Who better to raise your children than the elders with the knowledge and passion to do so?'

'These things and more you can achieve through commitment to the values of a social democracy. Please do not waste the opportunity you have as leaders of your community to achieve your fullest potential.'

These were his words, and the grand master went on to answer many other questions, but to conclude, he said this to the assembly:

'If not you, then who? If not now, then when? The future is yours to create.'

The law of the jungle:

Can you imagine – walking down the street, amongst the bustle of people, and accidentally bumping into somebody - being subjected to an absolute tirade of abuse and obscenities from the offended individual? What about driving your car and inadvertently cutting someone off in the traffic, then being assaulted by wild gestures, threats of intimidation, and a spectrum of obscenities that stretch the imagination? How about walking down the street and espying a good-looker only to leap upon him or her with unrestrained and untamed promiscuous intent?

Now, fortunately, these abhorrent actions, whilst they do occur within our society, happen only as a very small percentage of the many daily inter-personal relations among civilised human beings. Fortunately, we have learned how to negate or suppress our primal instincts, those uncivilised urges, and to conform to the standards of a civilised society. Free and unrestrained, these primal instincts would transform our society into the 'law of the jungle'. Our very presence at any particular place and time would require an alertness of mind and body just to survive. Indeed, it must have been much like that for the survivors of the Holocaust – a horrendous part of our historical record that occurred only seven decades ago.

For the most of the time, we are able to keep our emotions in check. We refrain from acting upon our baser instincts. We temper, avoid or ignore the powerful feelings of anger, jealousy or fear. Yet, as described in Chapter Twelve and more fully in Chong (2011) repression of the baser emotions is not the answer. According to Ben-Shahar (2008)

> ... it is not only our psychological well-being that is influenced by our emotions, but our physical well-being as well. Since emotions are both cognitive and physical – affecting and being affected by our thoughts and physiology – suppressing emotions influences both the mind and the body.

So what happens? Where do these base emotions go? If suppression or repression is not the answer, what do we do with them?

The answer, I believe, resides in PTF - 'permission to feel'. By acknowledging the presence of our raw emotions – to accept that we feel angry, irate, jealous, anxious or upset, is to give ourselves the permission to feel these emotions, but according to Ben-Shahar (2008) this simple permission, " ... to experience one's emotions does not only make the physical symptoms go away; it alleviates the negative feelings as well."

In addition, I would emphasise the need to release these negative feelings and emotions – go and meditate by a waterfall and let your feelings flow downstream, talk it out with a trusted friend or counsellor, or shed a tear, or express your baser emotions by writing in a journal. But please – do not 'hang on to them'.

… let's go back to the pond:

Over the ensuing months, both Monique and Gabriel had grown to know one another more intimately, not just in a physical sense, but to really know each other in every sense of the word. They got to know their individual habits and eccentricities, their thoughts and behaviours, and above all, their feelings and emotions. Then, through this understanding, their love continued to blossom.

Their usual habit was to get up about 6 o'clock in the morning and begin preparations for their daily activities. Monique would prepare for her work as the leader of the library and Gabriel had fast become involved with numerous activities relating to the youth of the pond … but more of this later.

This particular morning, Monique raised her head off the pillow and immediately felt an irresistible urge to be ill and, with haste, sped to the bathroom where she promptly regurgitated her last evening's meal. In a flash Gabriel was by her side in support and concern.

Noticing that Monique's face had gone a lighter shade of pale, Gabriel said, 'Let's get you to a doctor, shall we?' So they busied themselves in an effort to get to the nearest clinic.

'Well, what's the prognosis?' asked Gabriel, as Monique returned from the doctor's room into the waiting area.

'Well my love,' said Monique, 'you know how we mentioned before that we don't do things by half measures.'

'Yes,' was the cautious reply.

'Well, I'm pregnant.'

Gabriel looked at his wife with what can only be described as unrestrained joy. He let out a 'whoop', turned to the old drake sitting in the waiting room and said, 'I'm going to be a dad'.

The old drake, only partially amused said, 'Bully for you pal, I've got seven of them and I was de-nutted years ago'.

Then, not really hearing the old drake anyway, he proceeded to usher his partner to the nearest chair.

Monique managed to get Gabriel to sit down and stop pacing about, and then she said, 'But wait, there's more!'

'Huh? What are you talking about?' was Gabriel's confused response.

'We're expecting twins.'

Gabriel's response was to faint.

On the way home, after she stuck some smelling salts under Gabriel's nose, he and Monique walked arm in arm, animatedly discussing all the things that they would do now, and all the changes they would make to greet the arrival of the first two of their flock.

... some weeks later:

Gabriel was sitting under a tree, surrounded by a number of young teenagers. Over the past few weeks he had gone all out in an effort to better understand the needs of the younger members of the pond community. He walked amongst them, asked them questions and sought their ideas and feedback. All this, it must be said, with a mind in a state of euphoria over the pending approach of parenthood. In fact, he shared much of this with the young people he spoke with, who teased him unmercifully about his progress into parenthood. Gabriel took all of the banter with mild amusement and continued to delve into the world of the teenager, seeking as always, to lessen his ignorance of their characteristic behaviour and ideas.

This day he asked the assembled group to tell him what they really wanted to do with their lives, then, having posed the question, proceeded to listen attentively to their thoughts.

A young lass was the first to speak.

She said, 'You know, we are forever being told by our parents what they think is good for us. My Dad wants me to be a lawyer. To go to university and study hard then get a job in his law firm. But me, all I want to do is paint. I love the idea of painting things, to bring a canvas alive with all those colours and hues.'

'Yeah, I know what you mean,' said another lad named Brodie, 'my Mum is forever at me to get a job and I'm sure it's just because she wants me to start paying some of the rent. My mate, Nicholas, has a mother who is exactly the same.'

Another of the group said, 'Man, I just don't know what I want to do. I kind of just like hanging with my mates and cruisin'. You know what I mean?'

Gabriel catalogued these responses in his mind, along with all the other information he had accumulated, and then proceeded to ask the teenagers a 'permission' question.

He asked them, 'Guys, if I was a genie and if you could ask of me one wish, one thing that I would automatically grant you, what would that be?'

You could see the wheels turning inside the young people's minds. Indeed, there was a considerable delay of thought, but then, the young lass spoke her mind.

'Genie, I would ask that you give every duck in our pond happiness.'

Then the next young lad said, 'Genie, I would ask that you grant all of us teenagers the ability to make this pond the very best place to live.'

Finally, the next young lad said, 'Genie, I would ask that you grant all families of the pond the ability to live together in harmony.'

At these words, Gabriel stood up and stretched out his wings so that he best impersonated the majesty of a genie.

'Young children of the pond,' he said in his best genie-like voice, 'why do you ask me to grant you these wishes? For truly I say to you that it is within your capability to achieve these things yourselves … why do you need me?'

'But genie,' said the young lass, 'we are only teenagers. It is the older ducks that run things around here, we only get to do what they say.'

'Young children,' continued the genie, 'what the older ones

from your pond most need is the inspiration, motivation and energy that you have, to achieve all of those things you have requested. Without your passion, they can only do what they think is best for you. But if you demonstrate your drive and commitment, they will listen to you. Be free with your ideas, be determined with your resolve and do not be turned away by the naysayers. It is you who are the future of this pond. It is you who will be responsible for this pond's wellbeing … do not shirk from this responsibility, for I tell you in truth, what you seek for yourself in life, you should create for another. This will be your greatest boon.'

After these words, Gabriel sat down again, only to see the teenagers with eyes wide and mouths agape at what they had just witnessed and heard. Then, to break the spell, Gabriel said, 'Does anyone here know how to change a nappy?'

Chapter 16

We manifest in our life those events that will cause us to experience ourselves as who we really are.

Victor Frankl spent some years in a Nazi concentration camp. As a description of his life experiences as a Holocaust survivor where internment and extermination were common companions he wrote:

> The consciousness of one's inner value is anchored in higher, more spiritual things, and cannot be shaken by camp life. But how many free men, let alone prisoners, possess it?

and quoting Nietzsche, he continued:

> "He who has a *why* to live can bear with almost any *how.*"
> Viktor E. Frankl, *Man's Search For Meaning, (1959)*

Some perennial questions have been asked across the millennia:

> Who am I really?
> What is my purpose in life?
> What is the meaning of life?
> Why am I here?
> When this life is all over, what then?

These questions, and their like, have challenged the great minds of philosophers, religious leaders, and spiritual masters for many millennia. They are questions of great profundity and complexity and they have stretched the limitations of even our greatest minds through the centuries of our evolution.

But, how can we say that we manifest in our life those events that will cause us to experience ourselves as who we really are? When one considers the depths of man's capacity to abuse and mistreat his fellow man, how is it possible to say that we 'manifest' such inhuman experiences in our life? We only to have to remember atrocities such as the Holocaust and September 11, 2001, to name but two, where man's treatment of his fellow man gives rise to events of the most horrendous kind. Surely it defies belief and any sense of credulity to say that we manifest these kinds of experiences in our life!

Perhaps these questions are a means by which we can test the significance of our search for meaning in life? Maybe we should let a story tell a story.

A Story: Out of the Mouth of Babes

The old grand master was lying in his bed, almost near death. He struggled for breath and his every movement seemed to take an effort that led him further towards his end. There was much lamenting, for gathered around him were the many acolytes and monks that had been in his service for several years. Their tears flowed freely while lamentations and chants resounded clearly from the main assembly area and numerous other halls within the abbey; all came from those who did not have access to the grand master's chambers.

Of a sudden and completely without warning, the grand master raised his head from the pillow. It was as if some magical essence had filled his ailing body with such strength that he could master that feat.

'Go and fetch me the young novice, Michael,' was his tremulous command.

'But grand master,' said his principal assistant, 'he is but a first-year novice. He has been with the abbey only a few weeks. You are surrounded here by your monks and initiates.'

'Do as I say,' was the stern command. 'Quickly! Make haste,

there is not much time.'

So a messenger was dispatched to retrieve the young novice from his dormitory.

Some minutes later, and somewhat out of breath, the young novice was ushered into the chamber in which the grand master lay. He was no more than ten years old and still had not undergone any of the rigorous training in the austerities that define the life of a monk.

'Come, come to me young minion. I must speak with you. Come over here by my side.'

The novice took tentative steps towards the ailing master and knelt by his bedside in awe of his power and wisdom.

'Raise yourself, young man. I have not the strength to bend down to look at you.'

Then the master held out his frail hand for the novice to take.

'Come, take my hand.'

The novice did so, but the quizzical look upon his countenance was enough to assure the assembled acolytes that this situation was completely without plan or design.

Then, in wavering voice, the grand master said, 'Young novice, what is the meaning of life?'

At these words the novice looked aghast at the grand master, then said, 'But master this surely is a question for your monks, not a novice like myself.'

'Yes, yes, I know, but I want *you* to tell me.'

'Well master,' said the novice, 'I am a child of God. It is by His grace that I have this life, but it was my choice that I chose this life. I chose this body and this life so I could best realise my true self.'

'And, young novice, what of your life so far, how has it been?'

'Master, my life so far has not been without trial. I have experienced some pain, but I have also experienced much happiness.'

'And for what reason do you think that you have had these

painful and pleasurable experiences?'

'Well master, I guess it is because through these experiences I can realise my pathway to God.'

'Thank you, thank you, young man,' said the grand master softly to the novice, 'you will make a great master one day.'

Then, he addressed all who were assembled to hear his words.

'Listen well to the words of this young novice, for these are the words of innocence, untainted by a longing for redemption. He knows not the fear of death, yet he speaks the words that define our life. Harken to his words I say, and let none here deny their veracity. For truly, it is the young and the innocent who hold the key to the most profound questions about the meaning of life.'

At these words the grand master closed his eyes, and —with the most beautiful expression on his face – passed on to the next realm.

... and we return to the ducks:

The next months passed quickly for both Monique and Gabriel with both of them totally immersed in the activities of their chosen profession. For her part, Monique's experiences of pregnancy were not without the odd day of challenge, but for the most part, these challenges were considered a normal part of the process. That is, until a day some nine weeks before the scheduled due date.

'Gabriel,' she said upon awakening in the early hours of the morning, 'there is something wrong. I'm feeling painful contractions – I think the babies are coming' and her face contorted in pain as an agonising contraction grasped her inner being.

Gabriel shot out of bed, and with a quiet sense of urgency born of concern for his mate, made all the essential preparations to take Monique to the hospital.

The next few hours for Monique were spent in paroxysms of pain. Waiting in the corridor of the hospital made Gabriel feel totally anxious, despite his well-established reputation for serenity. He could hear the cries of his mate, but was denied access to the delivery room where Monique was surrounded by a team of dedicated doctors and nurses.

Each moment passed as an eternity. The clock on the wall of the waiting room seemed to have lost its tock. The hands appeared to be static and cemented in place. Hours later, the doctor appeared from the delivery room. Gabriel rushed to him.

'What has happened? Is Monique okay? What about my children, are they okay?'

The look on the doctor's face displayed a tired compassion. He tried to force a smile to his lips, but his brain seemed confounded by mixed emotions.

'Gabriel, Monique is fine. She is exhausted, but she will be okay. She will need lots of rest in recovery, but she is a strong duck with plenty of spirit.'

'Yes, and what about the twins, are they okay?'

At this question, a shadow seemed to pass over the doctor's countenance, but all at once, he recovered his professional demeanour.

'The twins have been born significantly premature; they have not had sufficient time to grow and develop in the womb as would ideally be the case.'

Gabriel's hands went straight to his face and his efforts to refrain from crying were a test to his inner resolve. In the pit of his stomach, he began to dread the doctor's next words.

'Both of your children have survived the birth, but are currently on life support to help them progress. We are doing our very best, but both of them will need a good deal of assistance over the coming days and weeks to help them pull through.'

The emotions that traversed Gabriel's gentle face at that time were too many and too varied to describe, but he managed to stammer, 'Can I see Monique? Can I see my children?'

'Yes, you can, but not for very long.'

And the doctor ushered Gabriel into the room in which his

beloved lay with tubes attached to her arm. His children were in two glass humidicribs, both of which had a multitude of tubes and regulators connected to monitors and meters.

He immediately rushed to the bedside of his partner and began to caress her cheeks. At once his tears began to flow unrestrained, and Monique's eyes opened wide. Then they immediately took on a sparkle born of her immense love for her life's partner.

'My beautiful drake, do not cry so. All is as it should be according to the divine. You are here, I am okay, and we have been blessed with our children.'

Gabriel's tears continued to flow. His normal eloquence had deserted his tongue at this time of pure emotion. After a moment or two, some coherence returned to his mind and he said, 'The love I feel for you today cannot be measured by anything in this life — only by God's own sense of divinity. For each further day that I am blessed with life, I will know what true love feels like for another – for you and our children.'

'Go and see your children,' said Monique 'they are waiting to see their father.'

With a heart almost bursting with pain and pleasure, Gabriel, traversed the few metres over to the cribs that held both of his children. What he saw were two small fledglings, wrapped in swaddling clothes and connected with tubes that aided their breathing. What he felt in his heart was unrestrained love for the two minute creatures that had been given life by divine grace. Their eyes were not open, but he could feel the power of their determination to hold on to life. He could sense the strength of their spirit in their quest to retain what they had been divinely given. He held his palms to the outside of the glass and remained that way for some time, in an effort to pass on his courage and strength through the power of osmosis.

As Gabriel returned to the side of his beloved, he said to her, 'I think it is important that we find names for our two young fledglings. It is right and proper that they be gifted with names that befit their stature and presence. What do you say? Do you have names that befit a little king and queen?'

Monique closed her eyes for a few moments, as if in prayer and certainly in search of inspiration.

'He that is in the crib on the left shall be called after his great grandfather, Alfred. Our young girl in the crib on the right shall be named Verity, in honour of the love between her mother and her father.'

At these words, Monique closed her eyes and fell into a deep slumber. At the same time, the doctor returned to the room to usher Gabriel into the waiting area and allow the nurse to tend to the needs of the children.

'Go home Gabriel. There is nothing else for you to do here. Come back later this afternoon,' said the doctor. But Gabriel could not. Instead, he went in search of the small room that contained the hospital's chapel and he sat down and began to pray.

Man's search for meaning:

> "As far as we are able to understand, the only aim of human existence is to kindle a light in the darkness of mere being."
> Carl G. Jung, as quoted in Jeffares & Gray (1995)

Perhaps the problem is that we are asking the wrong questions. Perhaps we should not be asking, 'What is the meaning of life?' or 'What is our purpose in life?' Maybe these are the wrong questions. Perhaps we should be asking instead, 'What are you making of your life?'

Think! In every minute, every hour of every day, what are the right tasks and actions that give meaning to *your* life? What are the right actions that overcome the obstacles and challenges that *your* life presents? How do your actions best serve the meaning *you* give to life?

With these questions, however, there is no blueprint or template that defines the meaning of life for all of mankind. Rather, the meaning of life will be as different as individual fingerprints. The only commonality will be the very real nature of our individual experiences.

A story: What You Believe is True

A young child sat on the knees of his father as he was being told a story. This was the young lad's favourite time, for it was the time when he had the total devotion of his beloved father. At the same time each week, the two would sit in the comfortable old lounge of their quaint, but modest home on the outskirts of the town.

This day, his father read him a story of dragons and sorcerers. It was a tale of great deeds of heroism in the fight against an evil that had beset the land. It was a grand adventure and one the young lad would remember for the rest of his days.

When his father had finished reading the story, he closed the book and placed it on the coffee table next to the chair. The young lad then asked of his father, 'Dad, are these stories really true? Did these things actually happen?'

'Well my boy,' said his father, 'some would say that these stories are myths and legends. Others would say that they are figments of wild imagination. Then, even others would say that they are literal truths about events that occurred many centuries ago.'

'But Father, what do you say?' enquired the lad.

'Well, what I know is that whatever you believe is true.'

'Dad, I don't understand. What do you mean?'

'Well Son, in life whatever it is that you believe in, you actually make real. It is real for you. By believing it, you make it real.'

'So Dad, if I believe in the devil, then I make him real?'

'Yes, this is so.'

'If I believe in God, then I make him real.'

'Yes, this is so.'

'If I don't believe in anything, then life has no meaning.'

'Yes, my son, this is so.'

'But if life has no meaning, then what is our purpose for being here?'

'Exactly son, exactly?'

'But Dad, where do I find this meaning?'

'Son, what do you love most in the whole world?'

'Well, I love you and I love Mum and I love my sister, Elizabeth, and I really love our dog, Misty.'

'Good,' said his father, 'because the meaning of life has its origins in love. Love for others, as well as love for yourself. Therefore, would you treat me and Mum badly?'

'No,' replied the boy, 'I love you.'

'Would you treat Elizabeth or Misty badly?'

'No, I would not. I love them too.'

'Excellent, because your actions are in harmony with the meaning and purpose you give to your life. I think too, that you are well on the way to a rich and fulfilling life?'

'Why dad, how do you know?'

'Because I love you too Son, and so does your Mum – Elizabeth and Misty, too.'

… back at the pond (a week later):

Many hours were spent in vigil beside the humidicribs of the two young ducklings struggling for life. Monique had spent much of the week in hospital recovering her strength. Gabriel had alternately dozed and stayed vigilant in the chair beside the bed of his partner or seated beside the glass of the humidicribs.

After the week had passed, it was plain to see a trend in the wellbeing of both of the little ducklings. In the past week, young Alfred had begun to prosper. He had gained a little weight and was now able to breathe without the help of the regulator. His progress was noted by the medical attendants and well acknowledged by the two concerned parents.

Verity, on the other hand, was not progressing well at all. At least on two occasions during the week, the monitors called for urgent and specific attention to her needs. She was nearly lost on both of these two occasions. But she was a fighter. Both Monique and Gabriel, whilst deeply in distress at the plight of their daughter, were able to sense her great determination to stay with them. Tears flowed freely, to be sure. Both Monique and Gabriel cried in equal measure, each to console the other when their feelings became too poignant.

As the hour approached midnight one evening, when Monique and Gabriel had managed to get a little sleep, all of a sudden the monitor above Verity's crib sprang to life with an urgent alarm. Both parents rushed to the side of their daughter's humidicrib, but were summarily directed outside by the head nurse, as she and her team came to take charge of the medical intervention. The doctor followed soon after, rushing through the door while still putting on his medical attire.

The moments passed in agony for Monique and Gabriel. Time was at a complete standstill and all thoughts of anything else in their lives were as a speck of dust to the sun. They sat hand-in-hand, without saying a word, just staring into space. But when they could restrain their anxieties no longer, they paced up and down the floor of the waiting room.

After what seemed an eternity, the doctor came out of the room to speak with them. His eyes were red from fatigue and his face sallow and pale. It was as if he had been confronted with the limitations of his own powers. He seemed to recognise how much he knew, but this was tempered by how much he still had to learn.

'Gabriel and Monique, your daughter has a very tenuous hold on life. Even with all of our assistance, she cannot get enough breath into her lungs to fully sustain her needs. This, even in the short term will affect her capacity to live a normal life. In all likelihood she will have restricted brain capacity and multiple organ dysfunction. Her quality of life will be severely inhibited.'

The blood drained from Gabriel's face and he could feel Monique's hand tremble in his own. Her face was porcelain.

'What are our options, doctor? What do you suggest we do?' asked Monique.

'I believe it is time to decide whether to try and sustain her life such as it is, through our medical interventions. The outcomes from that are unlikely to be positive. Or, whether to turn off the apparatus and allow nature to take its course.'

Monique let out an anguished cry and Gabriel felt like he had received a hammer blow to his chest. It felt as if his heart had been rendered from his body. Monique could barely stand unassisted and it was Gabriel who said, 'Doctor, can we be given time to make our decision?'

'Yes, of course, but you must know that I cannot determine how much time remains.'

In a haze of grief and anguish, Monique and Gabriel walked down the corridor of the hospital and entered the little chapel to pray and discuss their dilemma.

For a while they both stayed in silence, each in a turmoil of their own. They both prayed to their God, but all they heard in return was a deafening silence.

Gabriel went up to the altar and placed his head on the cold stone symbol of their God.

'Take my life in place of hers, dear God. Take me, not her,' was his anguished cry.

But Monique could stand the anguish no longer and she ran out of the chapel and down the corridor, then outside into the cold night air. Gabriel lifted his head from the altar and yelled after her, but she was gone.

... about an hour later:

After an hour or so, Gabriel was as concerned about his partner as he was about his child. He had gone outside in search of her, but there was no trace. None of the attending staff had seen which way she went. Not really knowing what to do, he went back into the chapel to continue his prayers and lamentation for a situation that was by that time getting considerably worse.

All of sudden, Monique came bursting back into the chapel. She was red from exhaustion and her breath was laboured and gasping, but under her wing she held a book. It was *The Book of Mysteries*.

Immediately, she placed the sacred tome on the altar and opened the cover to reveal the pages. All of a sudden a breeze emanated from somewhere that made the pages flutter and dance. Then, as soon as the breeze had arrived, it promptly disappeared. The pages of the tome settled in their place.

Monique and Gabriel watched this wonder in fascination. They then walked, hand in hand, up to the sacred text to see what was written on the page.

It was a simple, single sentence and one that they had read before ... it said:

"What would love do next?"

They looked at one another and they both knew. At that very instant, they knew what they should do.

The parents walked slowly back down the corridor towards the room that held their beautiful daughter. They then walked into the doctor's office to explain what they had decided and the doctor merely nodded his assent and walked with them towards the room.

As both Monique and Gabriel stood beside the humidicrib that held their precious baby, they nodded to the doctor. He switched off the breathing apparatus and removed the tubing from Verity's body.

Both parents then lifted the little child out of her crib and cradled the small body in their arms. As they did so, a peace and tranquillity seemed to fill the room. It was a silence replete with nothing but love. Then, all of a sudden, Verity's eyes sprang open and she held the focus of both her parents. Truly, it was like looking into the eyes of God. All seeing, all knowing, and yet total innocence. It was a look that neither Monique nor Gabriel would ever forget.

Then, as if she knew that it was time to go, Verity closed her eyes and passed from this realm into the arms of her maker.

... a little while later:

Monique and Gabriel returned to the chapel to pray and also to retrieve *The Book of Mysteries* that was still open on the altar. They spent a few quiet moments in prayer, in their own world of silence - in communion with their God.

After some time, they opened their eyes in readiness to make their way back home, but before they left, they could see that the pages of *The Book of Mysteries* had somehow and once again changed to reveal more words of wisdom. The page read:

Behold I am your God Almighty.

It is from me that from all life springs, and to whom all life returns,

But you must know, that everything is life.

Do not be afraid, for I am not a judgemental God – this is the design of men who know not the truth.

Yet, it is a return to innocence that will be your most profound journey of life.

All who are innocent are the truest reflection of God on earth. Your children, your elderly and your sick will all return to me as true children of God, I AM.

Fear not for the departed, for they reside with me, as me, and know also that they reside in you, as you, for we are not separate – all are one in the spirit that I AM.

Seek all that you love in the silence where I, and they, will be found.

Call my name and I will be with you, call their name and they will be with you.

Love is your bond, and to love you will all return, for love is what I AM.

Chapter 17

The fact that nothing happens by chance means that there are no coincidences.

My uncle and I were brought up in an atypical home in Melbourne, Australia. The address was 47 Winchester Street, Moonee Ponds. It was a large house that contained upwards of three generations of my family, and we lived with my grandparents (my uncle's mother and father), in this home, for over fifteen years. After my grandfather passed away, the house was sold to a developer who proceeded to renovate it thoroughly and subsequently on-sell it after a couple of years. That was all some thirty-five years ago. The different generations of our family have since dispersed to all parts of the country, with my uncle (and I myself) now living in different areas of Cairns, Far North Queensland, a region about two thousand eight hundred kilometres north of Melbourne – close to four hours' flying time.

About a year ago my uncle was working behind the bar at one of the principal hotel resorts here in Cairns and one particular evening he got talking to a gentleman, visiting the region, who said that he lived in Melbourne. As you can imagine, this started a conversation about the city. My uncle stated that he had lived in a place called Moonee Ponds, to which the other fellow responded, 'That's where I live'. My uncle then said that he used to live in Winchester Street, just near the corner of Learmonth Street. 'I live in Winchester Street', exclaimed the other gentleman. My uncle then told the fellow that he used to live at number 47 Winchester Street … 'That's where I live', exclaimed the visitor.

This meeting, what was it? A random event, a complete coincidence, or just plain luck? Most certainly it was an event that defies any established laws of probability. Of all of the millions of people in Australia, of all of the vast distances between cities and regions, not to mention the time expanse of some thirty years, for that fellow to be standing at the bar of the hotel at the exact same time that my uncle was serving drinks – was that pure coincidence? Or was it a stroke of pure luck?

Gary Player, the famous South African golfer, once said, "The more I practice, the luckier I get." But increasing one's level of competency does not explain the randomness of the situation described above with my uncle. The increase in a person's competency at a particular art, sport, or profession merely increases the probability of success in that chosen field.

I am sure that each of us can describe some event or occurrence in their life that defies probability. These events can be as mundane as being late for work and missing a train, and then finding that a friend is passing by in their car at that exact same moment; or, more dramatically, being late for work and missing a train, only to discover that the train is later involved in a crash that kills several passengers.

Perhaps if we have the ability of extra sensory perception (ESP), or if we are able to read another person's mind, or predict the future through precognition or clairvoyance – then these attributes might enhance our ability to increase our luck, or improve the odds of coincidences happening. But these attributes, even if proven and real, do not form a part of the modus operandi of the general population. For the most part, each of us goes about our day-to-day affairs with a total lack of awareness of any of these aspects of divination or any metaphysical prowess.

What if, however, we consider that every moment is important, that no incident or event is inconsequential? In other words, that every action we take has a consequence. If we consider that it is our soul's purpose to find and fulfil its reason for being here on this earth (whatever that purpose may be), then we can speculate that there are no 'random' moments or coincidences, only events that compel us towards achieving our soul's purpose. Moreover, if we are consciously aware of what our soul's purpose *is*, then we become more aware of the events and actions that aid us in its realisation. Nothing is random, nothing is coincidental – everything is meant to be.

A story: You Are Where You Are Meant to Be

The master was walking along a mountain pathway one afternoon. He was on his way to a village where he had been summoned to attend to an old lady who was approaching death. From the reports that had reached his ears, the old lady was much in need of a kind word and wise counsel to soothe her fears of the hereafter. The report had also stressed the old lady's sense of urgency about this matter.

It was rare nowadays for the master to venture beyond the confines of his abbey, for it was common practice for him to send his cadre of helpers and initiates out to the remote villages to give support to the people. It also helped these monks to gain experience and increase their skills amongst the people. But there was something that compelled the master on this occasion to make the perilous journey himself to tend to the old lady's needs.

The path that the master traversed was particularly steep and the road narrow and circuitous, and despite the robust state of the master's health, he still felt the strains of exertion in his legs and the labouring of his breath.

All of a sudden, the master rounded a severe bend in the road, only to find that there had been a landslide that barred his path. The rocks and debris were piled so high that he could find no way around them, and there was a sheer drop on the other side. It was impossible to climb over the fallen rocks, as that would have resulted in more landslides and the strong probability of death.

The master sat down by the side of the road and began to

meditate. There was nothing else he could do at that instant, so his meditations were conducted in peace and contentment, without any unnecessary focus on his dilemma. After some short time, the master heard the sound of an approaching vehicle. Along with the sound of the engine, he also heard the banter of numerous voices accompanied by laughter.

The master was roused from his meditations by a band of soldiers being transported via truck, along the same route that he had chosen. As the truck stopped behind the wall of rock and debris, the commanding officer alighted from the front cabin and saw the master sitting contentedly.

'What has happened, my good man?' asked the officer.

'It appears that our progress has been impeded by the force of Mother Nature,' explained the master.

'Oh, don't worry, I'll have this landslide cleared up in no time.'

Thereupon, he gave some swift commands to his troops who set about removing the obstruction so that all might pass.

'And where are you headed?' enquired the officer.

'I head towards the local village, to counsel an old lady in need of help,' said the master.

'Well, that's exactly where we're going. Our orders are to guard the village from rebels that have been harassing the villagers. Hop in and we'll give you a lift. We'll have you there in much less time than you could ever walk,' explained the officer.

And so it was that the master was able to ride with the troops in the back of the truck. Coincidentally, he was able to counsel and calm some of the soldiers who were exceedingly anxious about the prospect of battle with dangerous rebels.

When they arrived at the village, the master felt fresh and rejuvenated and he gave thanks to the officer and bade good-bye to the new friends he had made. He then walked calmly up to the door of the old lady's house and knocked, only to find that the old lady was right behind him. She had just returned from the marketplace where she had been buying her provisions.

'Lucky you did not get here any earlier, master. I have been at the market all day and I would not have been here to greet you.'

'Come,' said the master, 'it is time for us to talk ...'

... and back to the pond:

There were days when Monique felt that her grief would overwhelm her. There were other days when she knew that everything was as it should be and that the bond of love between her and her child, Verity, came unconditionally from her daughter's place in Heaven.

Her life was also occupied fully with the new challenges of looking after her other child, Alfred, who had now developed to such an extent that he was able to be at home with his mother and father. He required regular check-ups at the hospital of course, but all in all, he was progressing much to the satisfaction of the doctors and his parents.

Once again, Monique had taken leave of absence from the library. Indeed, as it was a progressive organisation, the library's board of management had instituted a policy of maternity and paternity leave a number of years earlier. So it was little trouble to arrange for an appropriate temporary replacement to fulfil Monique's duties, allowing her in turn to comfortably take the time to rear her newborn child.

Gabriel, for his part, was already used to working unusual and flexible hours. It proved fairly easy for him to support his partner and roster relief times for Monique, particularly when her many motherhood tasks, not to mention sleep deprivation, threatened to overwhelm her. Nevertheless, it must be said that he too was often assailed by a profound grief for the loss of his beautiful daughter.

One evening, after young Alfred had been fed and bathed, then put down to sleep, Monique and Gabriel took some treasured time together to just sit by the warmth of the open fire.

'Gabriel,' said Monique, do you remember when we first met,

after my father's death? You said that the feelings of loss, sadness, anger and denial are all a part of the grieving process? And that all of these feelings are of great poignancy? Do you remember those words?'

'Yes my love, I do.'

'So then, after the loss of our daughter, how do you feel about what has happened?'

At this profound question, Gabriel closed his eyes for some time before responding.

'Deep in my heart, I feel a great grief, a grief that I think will be with me for the rest of my days. Yet, I do not find this grief to be debilitating.'

'Tell me more,' said Monique.

'What grows inside of me now is a great *meaning of love*.'

'But what is that — a *meaning of love?'*

'Well, love is the only way to grasp another human being in the innermost core of our being. It is the only way to be fully present and totally aware of the other being. My love for Verity gives me a meaning to love – a love that knows no limits and no boundaries. Through this love, I am becoming more aware of what I can become, and what I should become – what is yet to be realised. Maybe, this was the purpose of her short life with us – for us to realise our own potentialities.'

'Yes, I too feel a great void in the core of my being, but maybe void is not the right word ... it is more like a, like a ...' as she struggled for the best word. 'It is more like a 'well' ... yes a well. But it is a well that is forever full of water, it can never be depleted and as I drink from the well, it is immediately replenished to the full again.'

'Hmm, my love, you are beginning to sound more like a philosopher than the ever-practical soul that I know and love.'

'Okay, so what now? Where do we go from here?'

'Hah, always back to the practical.'

'Yes, well, we do need to plan our way forward. To make ends meet, as well as fulfil our potential.'

'Alright,' replied Gabriel, 'I know that my pathway has three singular roads that must be travelled. I will traverse the road that supports the youth of our pond through the proper use of the Trust. This is a vital community undertaking, which I will fulfil. The second road is my commitment to our child. He deserves the very best efforts that a father can provide. This is a task I will undertake without wavering. The third is my devotion and love for you. I will never take you for granted, I will always respect you and together we will realise more than we ever could if we were alone.'

At these words, Monique went over to her life partner and embraced him – the profundity of the embrace spoke more to him than a thousand words ever could.

A Story: A Life's Purpose

The monk had just returned to the monastery of his upbringing. It had been many years since he had last strode the halls and traversed the uneven cobblestones of the courtyard. In those many years of his absence he had diligently pursued his dream, for this monk was not only an adept member of the brotherhood, he was also an artisan, a craftsman of the finest order. It had been his dream of many years to build a temple; it would be a temple of the finest workmanship and splendour. The monk understood that the building of this temple was more than a dream, it was his life's purpose – it gave meaning to his life and provided a fresh perspective to all of the trials he had endured along the way.

The monk was summoned into the chamber of the grand master of the abbey, not just to renew their acquaintance, but for the grand master to be brought abreast of all of the news of the monk's experiences.

'Grand master,' said the monk, 'it gladdens my heart to see you in robust good health and the monastery in such fine order

– as if nothing has changed.'

'Thank you my son. It also gladdens my heart to see you once again, but the lines on your face and the grey flecks in your hair attest to the trials that you have endured. Come, tell me your story. What has crossed your path since last you graced our presence here at the monastery?'

'Grand master, I have diligently followed my dream. It has taken over five years, but finally I have built my temple and what a grand edifice it is.'

'Yes my son, this is most glorious news, but I sense unease within you. A shadow casts itself upon your visage, as a cloud passes across the sun.'

'Master, it is true that I have built this magnificent temple, but it remains an empty shell – no one has come. The temple remains empty of devotees.'

'Hmm,' said the master, 'I can understand why your heart is troubled. But my good monk, answer me, 'Why did you build the temple?''

'Master, I built it so that people from all walks of life could come and share the blessings of the spirit with their God. To help make their lives more pleasurable and durable with the sparkle of grace that the temple can provide.'

'Yes my son, this is a divine purpose indeed, and do you believe that your every action, every stone and block that you laid was inspired by God.'

'Yes master, I most certainly do.'

'Then, firstly, you must allay your fears. Your temple is divinely inspired and your meaning and intent pure. You have built it - they will come, but you must be patient. Secondly, you must alter your craft.'

'Master, I do not understand. What do you mean, 'I must alter my craft'?'

'My son, your purpose in life is very clear and remains unaltered. You are also a master artisan and craftsman. To now fulfil your purpose you must alter your craft to that of orator. You must ring the bell of your temple, so that everyone can hear. Proclaim from the ramparts the divinity within the halls of the temple, for all to come and see. Live now the purpose of your life through the richness of your voice, rather than the dirt under your fingernails.'

'Yes master, I see. But where do I start, what do I do?'

'The first thing you must do, my son, is meditate. Then, in your meditations, you must listen for the divine words of inspiration that the universe will whisper in your ears. Then, when you hear the words, go forth with strength and fortitude for the pathway to your purpose will blossom anew. Finally, my son, you must remember, that with such a divine purpose, there are only actions of intent and events without coincidence. Nothing happens by chance.'

Chapter 18

If you believe in what you do, you do not need to fear anyone.

The Encarta Word English Dictionary (2011) has four descriptions for the meaning of the word, *Optimism*:

1 "The tendency to believe, expect, or hope that things will turn out well;
2 The attitude of somebody who feels positive or confident;
3 A philosophical doctrine, first proposed by Leibnitz, that ours is the best of all possible worlds; and
4 The belief that things are continually getting better and that good will ultimately triumph over evil."

Interesting! Yet Victor Frankl (2004) writing about his life in concentration camps, recalled an enormous and unexpected jump in the death rate:

"The death rate in the week between Christmas, 1944, and New Year's, 1945, increased in camp beyond all previous experience."

In his opinion, the explanations for this increase did not lie in

"... the harder working conditions or the deterioration of our food supplies or a change in weather or new epidemics. It was simply that the majority of prisoners had lived in the naïve hope that they would be home again by Christmas."

To be optimistic is certainly a preferable state of mind to being pessimistic. According to Ricard (2003),

> An optimist is somebody who considers his problems to be temporary, controllable, and linked to a specific situation. He will say: 'There's no reason to make a fuss about it; these

things don't last. I'll figure it out; in any case, I usually do.'

The pessimist, on the other hand, thinks that his problems will last ("It's not the sort of thing that goes away"), that they jeopardize everything he does, and are out of his control ("What do you expect me to do about it?").

I am sure we have all experienced being around a pessimist (or a group of pessimists). They certainly are difficult to tolerate aren't they? I've often found myself not wanting to engage or inter-relate with another person who continually displays an attitude of pessimism and negativity. Haven't you felt the same way? But can an optimists' positive perspective cause delusions about what is real and actual? Did the concentration camp inmates' assertion that they would be liberated by Christmas propagate thoughts of self-delusion contrary to the actual reality of their experiences? Perhaps the situation would have been vastly improved with an attitude such as, "I hope we are liberated by Christmas, but if not, that *will* happen sooner or later."

These are great dilemmas for us to consider and given that I have never endured the deprivations and horror of those who suffered during the holocaust, and I trust I never will, I can only surmise the extent of my own reactions if I were to be placed in a situation like that which occurred in Europe in the 1940s.

However, the question I now pose here is, 'Can we be better served? Is it preferable to have an optimistic outlook and an attitude of undeniable hope?'

One of the answers, I believe, resides in the term, "progress". Bayliss (2006) writes:

By hardwiring us with this drive for progress through improved partnerships, the universal power we call evolution, Mother Nature or God has endowed us with the means not just to survive but to prosper. This is the power-house of all our wellbeing; mind, body and soul. What's more, our inborn drive is not only for healthier relationships with people around us and the natural environment; we also have the drive to improve the harmony between our mind and body, our conscious and sub-conscious, and the relationship with ourselves.

The great thing about progress is that it is *measurable*. We can actually identify the quantum of how far we have come from the point at which we started. In my coaching workshops, I use what is called a 'progress and appreciation log' (PAPL). The purpose of this PAPL is for participants to review their goal (or goals) through the prism of:

- *What you said you were going to do* (identified goal-related actions);
- *What you did* (what actually occurred);
- *What you are going to do* (as actions towards the goal) – irrespective of what you have (or have not done) previously.

Within this consideration of *progress* lies the underpinning foundation of determined action towards a pre-ordained objective. The log also has the added benefit of eliminating or diminishing those extraneous influences that distract us from our designated purpose. These are things such as drugs like alcohol and nicotine, or an excessive need for amusement or self-indulgent entertainment - to name but a few of those influences that distract us from life's designated purpose.

The other essential ingredient for success, along with *progress,* is that of *resolve.* The important questions become:

- How much do you want this? (your objective or goal).
- How determined are you to persist in the face of adversity and negativity?

- When confronted by obstacles, how motivated are you to persist and to overcome?
- When you encounter a setback, how adaptable are you to 'change course' or 'try another strategy'?
- When the pessimist says, "You'll never make it", do you concur with them, or does this only increase your resolve?
- When the critic says, "That was a load of crap", do you dissolve in a paroxysm of grief and self-doubt, or do you learn from the feedback and improve your performance the next time?

Even under the weight of insufferable hardship, it is possible to pull through with meaning and purpose, a focus on progress, and a strong sense of resolve.

Does this sound like you? … I think it does.

… let's return to the pond (many years later):

The flecks of grey had only just started to appear around Gabriel's temples. In truth, though, it made him look rather distinguished, and his claim to be approaching middle age was still met with disbelief amongst many of the youth with whom he continued to associate.

For her part, Monique was even more regal than she had been in her youth. The years had a way of bringing forth a deep radiance in her being. She had the grace and easy ability to commune with the important and powerful, as well as the everyday folk of the pond, who were all frequent visitors to the library. Indeed, she was much loved by the community at large, and it was a challenge to find a single word said in malice against her.

The library continued its progress as a beacon for the known world of ducks. In fact, Monique was currently overseeing an extension to the library's original construction, one that would expand its capacity some twofold – a massive project to be sure.

For his part, Gabriel had been the catalyst for some marvellous innovations with and through the youth of the pond. Through his guidance and support, the combined youth of the pond had managed to establish a self-supporting centre of excellence for sustainable projects - to do with the reduction of fossil fuels in and around the pond. They had also established a centre of support for the prevention of youth suicides. This was a magnificent project, for not only did it have direct bearing upon the welfare of individual members of the community, but also by extension, the wellbeing of the entire community. It was also a model of collaboration between the elderly of the pond, and its youth; the wisdom and experience of the one group combined with the passion and enthusiasm of the other. Thirdly, Gabriel had managed to implement a method of restorative justice within the pond's legal system. This action was particularly effective in reducing the level of crime amongst the youth, as it brought offenders (many of them youngsters) into supervised contact with their victims. This system of restorative justice, building upon the existing pattern of retributive justice, focused on community service opportunities rather than incarceration. Gabriel and a committee of the pond's youth were actively lobbying drug and alcohol companies to help fund a programme of justice reinvestment, although, it must be said, that there was still some way to travel for them to break through the mire of self-interest and denial within those companies.

As for Monique and Gabriel, their love never wavered. In fact, it was plain to see for all who had even less than 20/20 vision, that they were as devoted to one another after all the intervening years, as they had been in the beginning.

One evening all three members of the family were enjoying a hearty meal, cooked by Gabriel, while they were discussing the content of their respective days. Monique spoke about her work on the new library extension, Gabriel about his exploits at the office of Acme Drug Company, trying to obtain their contribution to a justice reinvestment fund, and Alfred about his day at school.

After the meal was complete and the dishes stacked away, Gabriel said, 'You know what I'd like to do. I'd like us to look through some old photographs of our family. You know, the ones in the old albums.'

'Aw Dad,' complained Alfred, 'that sounds like a real drag.'

'Come on son, it'll be fun,' countered Gabriel, 'be a good lad and go upstairs to the attic and get out those albums of old photos from the chest. I think it's in the corner on the right as you go in the door.'

Alfred grudgingly did as requested, but, my goodness, he certainly took his time about it.

'What? Were you on go slow, young man?' exclaimed Gabriel as he saw his son descend the stairs, 'You certainly took your time.'

Alfred managed to ignore his father's friendly jibe and proceeded to carry a box containing a number of old photo albums under one arm, while under the other, he carried what looked like a leather scroll that was secured by a leather strap.

'What's this?' enquired Alfred. 'I found it amongst all the old cartons upstairs.'

'I actually have no idea,' exclaimed Gabriel. 'Monique, do you know what this is?' as he showed her the wrapping.

'Never seen it before,' said Monique.

Gabriel took the leather scroll over to the table and placed it under the light, then proceeded to untie the leather thong. As he unfurled the outer leather cover it revealed a letter. It was a handwritten letter.

'Alfred, its addressed to you,' said Gabriel, and at once a quaint smile delighted Monique's face as she saw that it was another letter from her great grandfather, also named Alfred. But this time it was addressed to another Alfred, her son. She also saw the first sentence of the first paragraph of the letter, and she almost burst into laughter. It read:

Dear Alfred,

Now don't let your parents read this letter to you. This is your letter, I am writing it to you, so you read it to them - go on lad ...

(So that is what young Alfred did).

I am your great, great grandfather, also named Alfred and when you look through the photographs in the albums, you will find an old photograph of me. You will notice that there is indeed some resemblance between you and me.

How do I know this, you may ask? Well, in truth, we are one in spirit and you are my blood, so the love between us is forever and eternal. I need only look into my heart to know that you are growing into a fine young duck. Worthy of the name you carry.

Within your heart, I am sure you are aware that you have been well served by your mother and father. They have spent their lifetime doing their best for you. Indeed, the love that binds you together is very strong – you chose your parents well. When their time on earth is done, it will be this love that sustains you through your trials and grief ... but this is for much later.

You are also probably wondering why I have written this letter to you - this *letter across time*? Well, in case you didn't know, I have written a letter to a family member of each of my following generations, and so, this is what I do for you. But, I say to you truthfully, that this letter is the most important. It is the most important because it brings news of prediction, as well as a call to preparation.

The times to follow, which we will call the awakening, will bring unprecedented challenges for your pond's community. Yours is the generation that is most affected by the actions of previous generations, by their profligate abuses of the earth's benevolence. For many years, generations of ducks have been attached to the illusion of separation. They believed only in taking for their own benefit. They were attached to being 'right' and thus causing many others to be 'wrong'. They were convinced of the 'goodness' of their actions, not realising that what was 'good' for them made many others 'wrong, bad or evil'. They believed in individual prosperity and not collective benefit, and they fostered division rather than inclusiveness – those that were not 'with' them, were 'against' them.

Their actions have consequences, as all actions do. Your Mother Earth cannot sustain such excess, and your divinity of purpose cannot be expressed under the weight of such polarity – therefore change must occur. For some, this will be called Chaos, for others it will be called Calamity. Some may even call it Evolution, but the really wise amongst you will call it Opportunity.

It is an opportunity to express your divinity – the divinity that is in each and every duck, not just a chosen few. To make the shift, you must make your choices by expressing your highest truth, through actions that reflect your highest good and greatest potential. Proceed by the providence of divine grace, to do that which is in your heart to express and fulfil. Yet, you must always remember that your greatest barrier to fulfilment will be the absence of humility.

In the face of the challenges of tomorrow, remember also – and do not fear it – that you are never alone, for you and the Divine are one. In fact, when you are clear on purpose, when your life is full of meaning, you need never be afraid. If your purpose fulfils itself in each of the precious moments of every day, then the highest questions you can ask in the challenging times ahead will be:

'Where do I need to be (in service to the divine)?' and;

'What choice reflects my highest purpose?'

The answers to these questions will lead you to your greatest potential - at all times - wherever you are. Remember to approach all challenges with an open mind, for if you think you know something, this closes the mind as to what is possible. Indeed, you must let go of what you know to find out what you still need to know.

Young Alfred, your parents are your rock and will forever be your guide. Treasure their love and know that it has no bounds. If you seek inspiration, this too can be found. But this time, turn to those who are considered the least useful amongst you – your children, the disabled, your sick and elderly. These are the ones who will provide you with the inspiration to serve the highest good.

My greatest fortune is to have realised that 'life is eternal', and so, this, the last of my letters across time will be the start of a great new journey for the history of ducks, and for you, my great, great grandson, the expression of your highest reality – who you really are.

Yours truly,

Alfred D. Duck

P.S. Look closely within the leather satchel in which you found this letter – you will find a secret pocket. Within this pocket you will find a sacred symbol. This is your treasure, and when the time is right, you will know what to do with it.

Chapter 19

Enter into the wonder that you are.

… Straight back to the pond:

Alfred quickly picked up the leather satchel and began examining it thoroughly. Both Gabriel and Monique, in their impatience, could scarcely refrain from taking the parcel from his grasp and undertaking the search themselves. After some moments, however, Alfred let out a 'Here it is,' as he found the secret compartment and removed the sacred symbol. It was small, about two centimetres in diameter and made of gold. It was of circular design and had, what appeared to be sacred carvings, resembling a double helix of some long-forgotten era etched ornately upon its surface. The outer rim had four, small rectangular notches at each of the four points of the compass. In the centre there was a small rectangular hole.

The three took it in turns to scrutinise the ancient artefact. Indeed, it was well into the night, each beset by the need to sleep, before they became resigned to the fact that they had no idea what the ancient symbol represented. They were each of the same mind however - to go straight to the library the very next day to continue their quest to uncover the mystery.

By the end of the next day, they were no further advanced in their understanding. They had consulted numerous ancient texts and the most recent scholarly papers in effort to find out the meaning of the symbol. They were disappointed and none the wiser for all their enquiries.

'Well son,' said Gabriel, 'I'm afraid that we are just going to have to allow time to be our teacher, for it seems that this symbol is a first. There appears to be no record of such a symbol appearing anywhere in our recorded history.'

'What are we going to do with it in the interim?' enquired

Alfred.

'Well, the symbol was given to you by your great, great grandfather and so, it should be your responsibility to maintain it in safety, until such a time as its meaning and its use is brought to our understanding.'

'Okay Dad, I will keep it under lock and key at home. I'll put it in the cabinet along with our other important papers and things.'

'Good thinking, my boy, but make sure you carry a key with you at all times. I have a feeling that the symbol's use will be demonstrated rather than understood.'

The Guru Factor:

I am a very fortunate man and have received many blessings in my life. Many I do recognise and acknowledge; many, with my limited vision, I probably do not even realise. Without any doubt, one of the most precious gifts I have been given is to have a spiritual master as my mother. She is a divine being, an adept, an initiate, some would call her a guru … although she refrains from using any of these terms to describe herself.

Every day, people come to see her to seek guidance and enlightenment and relief from their troubles. They come seeking wisdom and solutions to vexing life issues. My mother greets them all, without discrimination, judgement or favour. Her meditation classes are full of devotees. Some people have been in her circle for years, others have come and gone. Many who have come over the years have made great progress and realised their great potential, others are still 'stuck in a rut', yet they still come.

Indeed, it is a very great blessing to be in the presence of a divine master, a spiritual master or a guru. The recent passing of the great Indian spiritual master Sai Baba witnessed many thousands of devotees from around the world go into mourning. Just a precious moment in the presence of such divinity would be a life-altering experience, and yet, I can walk into my mother's home and say, 'Mum, what's for dinner.' Wow!

However, for me, seeking out a guru or a master, can be a great trap – a honey pot trap, if you will. We can be in the presence of divinity. We can bathe in their essence, delight in and rapture at their words and gestures. We can hang on to every word as a balm to our life's ills. If we are lucky, each time we confront a challenge or obstacle in life, we can go running back to their doorstep and seek comfort or ease from our problems. Hey, we might even seek solutions, so that the problem might be somehow, magically removed.

Yet, this is NOT the task of an enlightened being. This is not the role of a master. The role of the master is to not 'give you the light', for they cannot give you what you already have. The role of the master is enlightenment - 'En-lighten-ment'.

According to Walsch N.D. (2002), "Listen to no man who declares himself or herself to be more special than anyone else." Further, he states that, "If a man or a woman seeks to set himself separate and apart from the rest of humanity, or claims to a be higher or better or holier than the rest, by declaring themselves to be "more than" or "greater than" others ... run from them as fast as you can."

A story: Reflections in a Well

'But he is,' said the young novice most forcefully.

'No, he is not,' the other exclaimed, equally indignantly.

'But he must be,' said the first, I saw him place his hands on an old lady who was stricken by a malady, and behold she was cured.'

Then a third novice of a similar opinion said:

'I too saw him relieve a man of his burdens of pain. He was once beset by great pain, and then, by virtue of a touch to his forehead by the master, he was cured.'

'What do you have to say to this?' demanded the first young novice.

'I have no doubt that you saw the truth,' said the second in explanation.

'Then, you agree, our master is the greatest of masters. He has cured the sick and his blessings are a balm to the whole world,' said the third novice.

'Yes, you are correct my friends,' replied the second, 'our master is a great teacher, but your desire to see the miracles, shades your eyes from the truth.'

'What do you mean?' said the first angrily. 'I'll have you know that if you say one more word against our master, I will give you a rap with my staff.'

'Calm yourself, my friend, I mean no disrespect to our master. Yet all I say is that you confuse his role.'

'What do you mean?' said the third novice. 'Explain yourself, or I too will give you a rap with my staff.'

'Come with me,' said the second novice to the pair, as they walked over to the nearby well.

'Look into the well and tell me what you see.'

'I see myself,' said the first novice, 'I see my reflection.'

'Yes, that is so.'

'Now lean in and scoop out some of the water and splash it on your face.'

This the first novice did and the second asked him, 'How did that feel?'

'It felt absolutely wonderful. It was totally refreshing.'

'Hmm, now scoop out some water to drink. Refresh yourself.'

'That was great,' exclaimed the first novice, 'the water is so fresh and I was so thirsty. I know that water is like life. Without it, we die.'

'Yes, that is so,' said the second, 'but tell me, whose face did you see in the water?'

'It was mine,' said the first novice.

'Exactly,' said the second.

'But I do not understand. What are you trying to tell me?'

'Our master and the well are one. When you come to the well you come to quench your thirst and to refresh your being, but in truth you seek these balms from yourself. You are the well. Its divine essence, the water, lies within you. The role of the master is to lead you to this realisation – to lead you to your well. The difference between you and the master is that, the master sees no separation between you and him, while you see the master as someone other than yourself.'

… Let's return to the pond:

Over the ensuing months, Gabriel had returned to his work amongst the youth of the pond and continued to make significant progress within the numerous projects he had initiated. For her part, Monique oversaw the mammoth task of the construction of the library extension. Indeed, it was only a few weeks away from completion.

One particular evening, Gabriel and Monique were enjoying a conversation beside the open fireplace that gave off a pleasant warmth to counter the chill of the evening. Alfred was in his room studying purposefully, he hoped, for some forthcoming exams.

Gabriel mused, as he took a quiet sip of his favourite red wine.

'My love, why is it that we have been so lucky to have a love that has endured, indeed prospered over all of these years?'

'My good drake,' said Monique, 'luck has nothing to do with it. There is nothing random about the endurance of love. Nor does it conform to any laws of chance or probability. If anything, it is more to do with wonder than chance.'

'Whatever do you mean by 'more to do with wonder than chance'?'

'Well, to wonder is to remain in awe of something beautiful or new, isn't it?'

'Well, yes, sure but …'

'Well, I will never forget the depths of my loneliness and the limitations to my potential before I realised you would be my soul mate. It was like having '*un coeur en hiver*', as the French say, 'a wintry heart'. From that time on, each day has been a wonder, a miracle of renewal. Through all of the good times and also through the more challenging. Even the days when you managed to really 'piss me off'.'

'Hmm, I see your point, you most practical of creatures, and although the convoluted depths and cryptic, multi-layered complexity of a duck's heart is far beyond the mental acuity of most drakes, it does appear that my heart concurs with your own.'

Suddenly, as they were both sitting once again in silence, the house began to shudder. It was but a minor thing at first, but then after a few moments, it became far more menacing. The figurines on the mantelpiece and pictures on the wall began to fall and smash on the floor. There was an almighty roaring sound, like a bomb going off, or an explosion. The ground was shaking and the pair found it hard to keep their footing.

'Quickly,' screamed Monique, 'go and get Alfred! The house is about to collapse.'

As Gabriel was ascending the stairs to Alfred's room, he was met half way by his son, and the look on his face attested to his level of panic.

'Dad, what's going on?'

'I don't know son, but we've got to get out of here, we're dead if we stay inside.'

At that very same instant, the floor supports of the house gave way and the staircase they were on collapsed under them and the roof started to cave in – there were bits of roofing and furnishings flying everywhere.

Gabriel grabbed hold of his son's outstretched arm and wrenched him back in the general direction of the lounge room where he had last left Monique.

'Monique where are you?' he screamed above the noise of the tremor. He couldn't see anything, for all the lights had gone out and there was a pallor of choking dust in the air. Not hearing a response, he grabbed hold of his son and screamed, 'Quickly get outside onto the street. Wait for me there, I've got to find your mother.'

Gabriel frantically shoved his son out through what was left of the front entrance and then ran back into the house in search of his soul mate.

'Monique, Monique, where are you?' he yelled into the cloud of dust and debris.

But there was no answer. He scrambled over broken furnishings and stumbled between fallen rafters. From the corner of his eye he noticed that a fire had started and was gathering pace amongst the tinder and broken shards of wood. Struggling to make his way back into where he thought was his lounge room, he tripped over what must have been the remains of his old display cabinet and he hit his head on some sharp protrusion. Blood poured from the gash in his forehead and he could barely retain his senses as blood poured into his eyes and down his cheeks.

Once more he yelled, 'Monique where are you?' and at this, he heard a faint murmur – barely audible above the clamour and the sound of the hastily engulfing flames that were gathering energy and power. With superhuman strength, coming from an unknown source, he lifted beams and broken furnishings. Then, all of a sudden, he felt the soft hand of his lover – she was lying prone, trapped under the weight of a roof beam.

'Monique, I'm here, I'll get you out,' and he strove with all his might to lift the large beam that had felled his dying partner.

Then, as if a silent space had carved itself out of the clamour and mayhem, he heard Monique say, 'Its okay – I'm going home now,' and he at once felt her hand grow limp and lifeless … she was dead.

It was then that Alfred, who was outside in a state of panic and desperation, heard a piercing wail arise from the very depths of Gabriel's grief and despair. Then came an almighty roar as what was left of the roof of their house collapsed and caved in, and the fire engulfed the remains of the building. His mother and father were still inside.

A (final) Story: It's Time to Go

The old master was strolling down the road along with his small retinue of novices. This was a pleasurable time for all of the young devotees, for they were able to commune directly with their wise old master, and also enjoy the pleasures of the afternoon sun and the cooling breeze that refreshed their energies. Indeed, this had become something of a habitual event for the group, for once a month they got to commune with nature and each other outside of the temple, freed from its spiritual rigours. Even the old master seemed to enjoy the casual banter among the young devotees.

As they were strolling along on this particular day, the old master suddenly became very solemn as he spoke to his group of followers.

'My young novices, I tell you in truth that I will soon be leaving this earth and passing on to the next realm. I am an old man, and my time on earth is nearly done.'

At these words, there was much lamenting and many wails of sorrow. Some of the young novices collapsed upon their knees and moaned uncontrollably. Another grabbed the hem of the master's cloak and sobbed inconsolably into the folds of the garment.

'Do not leave us, master,' said one.

Another cried, 'You are our guiding light, you cannot leave us now, not when we are yet to attain our own masterhood.'

But then there was one, who shed no tears and who seemed to be aloof from the distress of the others.

'Master,' he said, 'your parting from us will bring us great sorrow and grief, yet the cows will still keep on bringing milk,' as he pointed to a cow on the hillside. 'And the hawk will continue to fly in the sky,' as he pointed to a hawk circling amongst the clouds.

The master fixed his stern gaze upon the outspoken young novice and said, 'Will they? How can you be so certain that the cow will continue to provide in abundance and the hawk continue to soar in flight?'

'Master', said the somewhat perplexed novice, 'I say this because it has always been so.'

The master raised himself to his full height and a power beyond all rational understanding emanated from him.

'You,' pointing sternly at the now frightened boy, 'are deluded by your excessive pride and hubris. You think that no matter what you do to our Mother Earth, that she will continue to provide you with her abundance. Your lack of humility is an example of how we have brought Mother Nature to her knees. Have you not seen the patterns of weather changing and the seasons becoming confused? Are you not aware of the storms and tempests that rage with ever increasing ferocity and frequency? Do you not realise that the cow on the hill that you pointed out to me has not given such a quantity of milk this season, because the rains have not replenished the grasslands? Are you not aware of the hunger of the hawk because the rabbits have died from the poison in the land? ... and you dare say to me that things will always be the same.'

'Master,' said the now chastened boy, as he fell to his knees. 'I am sorry. My ignorance has blinded me to the truth of things. What must I do to atone for my sins?'

'Ignorance is not a sin, my son, it is merely ignorance, but now, through your enlightenment, you can best serve the purpose for which you were put on this earth.'

'Master, I will do whatever I can to fulfil my purpose.'

'Good,' said the master, 'come with me.'

Whereupon they walked briskly over to an old farmyard, just off the track that they were traversing.

'Young novice, take that axe, then go and chop down that old sapling over yonder,' said the master to the still chastened young fellow.

So the novice did as he was asked, and chopped the old sapling down.

'Good, now chop this wood into kindling and logs for a fire.'

So this is what the novice did.

'Good, now go and give these logs and kindling to the old farmer and his wife.'

So the novice duly complied.

'Excellent, now go into the farmer's shed and retrieve the potted sapling that is by the side door.'

The novice did as he was ordered.

'Good, now plant this young sapling next to the spot where you chopped down that old tree.'

Again, the novice did as commanded.

'Excellent, now say a blessing over the young sapling and give thanks to Mother Earth for providing wood for the farmer's fire.'

This the novice completed.

By this time, it must be said, the young novice was sweating profusely from his exertions, but he managed to gasp, 'Master, why have you got me to do these things?'

The master then assembled the entire group of novices around in a circle and said to them, 'You see that mother earth provides in abundance. She will continue to give until she can give no more. She provides wood for our fire and food for our stomach, yet her abundance cannot be sustained unless we give back to her what we take from her. We cannot continue to take her riches without giving back, and giving thanks. This is a fundamental law of nature. Moreover, if we continue to poison our lands, our rivers and the air we breathe, she cannot give to us what we most need for our survival.'

At these sage words, all of the assembled novices fell to their knees in homage to the master's wisdom.

Then the master said, 'Today has been a great lesson for you all. Go now and spread this message to all who have ears to hear. Tell them that our Mother Earth is in dire need of our succour and it is we who must come to her rescue. Do not be put off course by the naysayers, for it is only ignorance and pride that prevents them from hearing. This message is too important to be put aside, for we will all suffer the consequences of inaction and denial.'

'If you do this,' continued the master, 'I will pass to the next realm knowing that our mother earth is in safe hands.'

Growing old is a relative experience:

The stark reality of life is that we grow older every day. Now this will not come as a shock to anybody, nor will the wisdom of such a proclamation trouble many eminent thinkers. Growing old, however, is a subject worthy of much more subjective consideration.

With the progress of age, our physical body goes through significant permutations of the aging process. Hair goes grey, body muscle diminishes and our skin becomes less supple than it once was in youth. Not to mention the effects of illness or accidents suffered in the intervening years. Much can be said about each of these characteristics of ageing. I would, however, much rather take note of what we have right throughout our life and which is in complete abundance – and that is our attitude.

Growing old and gaining maturity are certainly not to be expressed through attempts at looking younger. It is not about dyeing our greying hair, or injecting chemicals to temporarily minimise wrinkles – far more important is that we maintain an attitude of youthfulness. This may mean that we retain a curiosity for learning new things, whether they be physical, emotional, intellectual, or spiritual. It could mean that we maintain an attitude of cheerful optimism and an unwavering sense of life's purpose. It could mean that we continue to explore new areas of passion and interest. It may also mean that we maintain an attitude of vigilant attention to a cause or a societal issue.

So, the mantra becomes:

"Don't grow old gracefully – grow old with attitude."

Let us return to the pond (for the last time):

The morning light brought a stark reminder of the events of the previous evening. Alfred was curled up in a foetal position outside of what remained of his family home. His hands were covered in soot and ash and his face showed rivulets where his tears had made causeways down through the grime on his cheeks. He was cold and shivering in the chill morning air. There was nothing left of the house except rubble and broken beams, although the brickwork fireplace stood like a sentinel amongst the ruins. In the background he could hear sirens wailing and he could see at a distance the flashing neons of emergency service vehicles, as well as some fires that remained ablaze.

Hungry, and with as much pure emotion as without conscious thought, he scrambled through the broken beams and rafters of his home in an effort to locate his parents. He knew they were dead. There was not even a filament of hope in his heart that they might have survived – yet he continued to dig through the rubble.

As he lifted a beam from the area that he thought resembled the living room, he saw the glint of something metallic that reflected in the early morning light. He reached in between some broken timber and shards of glass and what he retrieved made his heart skip a beat – it was the golden symbol that his great, great grandfather had bequeathed to him. Despite a little dust, it looked relatively unscathed. Brushing it up against his cloak, he put the sacred symbol in his pocket to work out later what he would do with it.

At that same moment, an emergency services vehicle came weaving up the road, taking care not to make contact with the great rifts in the roadway or the considerable debris that littered the street. At once, seeing the plight of the young man, an emergency worker came up to Alfred to ask of his plight.

'My parents are in here. I must find them,' yelled Alfred, who at once started to cry.

'Come on son, you come with me,' said the emergency services worker, 'we'll find your parents for you,' and he took Alfred's hand and led him to the back of the ambulance to tend to his cuts and abrasions and place a warming blanket around his chilled body. He then got on the radio, describing the situation and called for additional help.

The shock was now too much for Alfred and he began to tremble and shake uncontrollably, whereupon the ambulance officer gave him a sedative to calm him down. Alfred fell into a deep slumber.

Many hours later he awoke in a strange bed with a drip attached to his arm. Waking with a start, he immediately tried to detach the drip from his arm and raise himself from the bed.

'I've got to find my parents,' he yelled.

Instantly a nurse came to his side and made efforts to calm his anxieties.

'I will try to find out what has happened to them,' said the nurse soothingly.

About an hour later a police officer entered the ward in which Alfred was still resting.

'My boy, are you the son of Monique and Gabriel?'

'Yes, yes I am. Are they alright? I want to see my Mum and Dad?'

'I'm sorry to tell you, but your mother and father are dead. They were killed in the earthquake that flattened your house.

Their bodies have been taken over to the courthouse which is being used as a temporary morgue. I am very sorry for your loss.'

Alfred just kind of looked at the officer, without really seeing him, and then just stared into space. After the officer had left, the nurse returned to his bedside. She took Alfred's hands with a great compassion. The tears began to well in his eyes and soon became floods of grief and sorrow that shook his thin body with great tremors and waves of unrestrained emotion. There were no words exchanged between the two, but the nurse remained with him for a long time until his grief abated.

Two days later, Alfred's strength had returned and he was well enough to be discharged from the hospital. He made his way out of the double-front doors and out into the street. Not knowing where to go or what to do, he looked both ways down the street, only to see a trail of destruction that littered the once quiet streets of the pond.

Confused and alone, he didn't know what he was going to do, so he made his way to the courthouse in an effort to see the bodies of his mother and father. After going through the gut-wrenching trauma of viewing and identifying the bodies of his parents, he once again made his way out into the street in the glare of the midday sun that shone as if nothing was anything different from the day before.

He was hungry and needed to eat and at once felt inside his cloak to see if he had any money. His hand clasped around the sacred symbol.

'What on earth am I going to do with this?' he asked to himself.

All of a sudden he had what can only be described as an irresistible urge to go to the library – he needed to see *The Book of Mysteries*.

Having walked the few miles to where the library was located, all he saw when he arrived was a building that had been completely and utterly destroyed. It was a ruin. Very few of the beautiful balustrades remained standing, and a fire had engulfed much of the remains. Not surprisingly, the area had been cordoned off with police tape and there were a few security personnel patrolling the area.

Although he was aware he would get into trouble if he was caught, he knew he had to go and find the sacred book that once belonged to his great, great grandfather, and had been treasured by members of his family over many generations. He looked around and found an emergency services worker's coat that had been absent-mindedly left hanging on a nearby post. He put the coat on and began walking amongst the rubble, making sure not to attract the attention of the security guards.

By some compulsion, to this day unexplained, he made his way through the broken rubble, burnt books and shards of timber to an area that he thought most likely to be the repository of *the Book of Mysteries*. Then as much by inspiration as reasoning, he took the sacred symbol out of his pocket and held it up to the light of the midday sun. The ray that radiated from the sacred symbol was like a laser beam and it pointed a way straight to an area amongst the rubble. Alfred immediately began to dig. He lifted a large slab of timber and removed some broken glass – and there it was, *The Book of Mysteries*.

To his naked eye, it appeared that the book had remained unscathed. There didn't appear to be any external damage. He immediately looked around furtively to ensure that he had not been seen, and placed the book under cover and inside his cloak. By then making his way around the cover of a pillar, he managed to get out of the library precinct without being seen.

'What to do now? Where do I go from here?' he thought to himself and again, he felt the thud of inspiration in his guts. He made his way to the pond's old graveyard.

By the time he arrived, the mid afternoon sun had started to lose some of its force and the shadows lengthened as they fell upon the many gravestones that lined the area. Once again, this time as much from inspiration as anything else, he removed the sacred symbol from his pocket and held it towards the light. The laser beam that emanated from the symbol pointed directly to an old dilapidated gravestone about a hundred metres down the road. Alfred followed the trail.

As he knelt by the gravestone and wiped the mould and dirt from the headstone - this is what he read as the inscription:

Alfred D. Duck – b. December 25th 1904 – (there was no date of death)

Underneath, the epitaph read:

"There is no such thing as death – life is eternal."

Alfred then removed both *The Book of Mysteries* and the sacred symbol from his cloak and placed them on the gravesite. Then, all of a sudden the pages of the sacred book started to shake and the cover flew open with a loud thud on the grass of the gravesite. The leaves of the book began to flutter and, as if having a mind all of their own, settled at a particular page. This is what Alfred read:

'Behold, I am your God Almighty, and you are my treasured son.

This is the time of your great Awakening, and as such, is the greatest opportunity.

It is time to acknowledge that there is much about God, as yourself, that you do not yet realise.

It is the time for you to realise your own divinity – for you and I are as one.

What you now experience is the ultimate pathway of this realisation – but do not be afraid – you should never, ever be afraid.

What you are now experiencing is a manifestation of your old patterns of belief, about God and Life that no longer serve you well.

If you are now willing for new understandings about God and Life to be brought forth, this will be the new beginnings for life on earth.

If you are willing for your inner truth to emerge, this will also be the new beginnings for life on earth.

The first of all truths is that "all my children are one" – there is no separation between you and the divine, I AM. All are one on earth, as it is in heaven.

Fear not for your daily bread, for life is abundance and your mother earth will provide – if you stop taking without giving back.

Be ready, willing and able to follow your inner truth – I will always be with you, even unto the end of time.

The second of your truths is that life is not the "survival of the fittest", but rather the "collaboration between equals" – all of my children are blessed with a gift – every one of them so you must find it and use it.

If you ask me the question, "What is my purpose in life?" I will give you the answer. In truth, I answer all of your questions, always. It's just that you just do not always listen to the answer.

If you seek me, seek me in the silence of your heart, not in the logic of your mind. I will be the flower that blooms in your garden, the caress of the breeze on your face and the touch of your partner's hand in your own. I AM love, love is what I AM.

Seek your highest good through the expression of love for others, and even more, yourself.

Ask always the question, "What would love do next?" This is the pathway to the realisation of your highest potential.

You have been served by your ancient wisdoms and scriptures, but you must now ask the question, "Do they continue to serve me well?"

In truth, these ancient scriptures were ever there to help you realise your own truth – not to give you the truth.

Do not be fooled. In life, nothing happens by chance – everything is divine, but it is your choice what you experience with this divinity.

If you see all others as yourself, your divinity will ever be expressed for the highest good – this is a law of the universe.

Most importantly, remember that each life has a purpose, every life has meaning. The purpose and meaning are for you to realise. You will come to know who you really are – You and I are One.

I am your God Almighty, it is I that gave you the gift of life. This is my greatest gift to you, but know that life is eternal — you cannot be separate from me in all of life, you can only think you are.

Go forth – express your truth and fear not, for I am always with you.'

As he read the magical words on this page, Alfred once again saw the pages of *the Book of Mysteries* flutter of their own volition … but this time the book opened to the very back inside cover. What he then saw took his breath away. He saw an indent, on the page that was the exact same size and replica of the sacred symbol that his great, great grandfather had given him. Immediately he knew what he should do.

Alfred aligned the ridges in the symbol with the space in the book then placed the symbol firmly into place.

All of a sudden a golden light shone from out of the back of the book. It was so bright that it almost blinded him. What he then saw made his heart beat beyond the confines of his chest. The book was getting bigger – the number of pages was growing. The book was growing. At once there was double the number of pages that were there before. 'It was some kind of miracle,' Alfred would explain when he later told the story to all that would listen.

When the bright light had diminished and Alfred was able to see, in plain daylight, what had actually happened, he saw that in the middle of the book was now a mirror. When he looked, he saw his own reflection. It was his reflection – and yet it was not. It was himself, but without the bags under his eyes, or the dirt encrusted on his cheeks, or the first grey feather he had noticed a few days ago. It was if he was looking at his 'true' self. 'Man, this is some kind of miracle,' he said to himself.

The remainder of the pages were blank, there was nothing written on them, except for the top of the first new page. It said … 'This is YOUR story now.'

Alfred then felt the loving touch of his parents by his side. He was no longer afraid. He knew what he had to do.

He took the sacred book and secured it safely within his cloak. He got up from the place next to the headstone beside which he had been sitting. He looked west, turned towards the setting sun, and he flew to where he knew not.

THE END

References

Baba, M, *Discourses*, Sherlar Press, USA, 1987

Bayliss, N. Dr, *The Australian Wish Magazine*, NSW, October 2006.

Ben-Shahar, T, *Permission to Feel*, Happiness and its Causes conference workbook, NSW, 2008.

The Bhagavad-Gita as it is, McPherson's Printing group, Victoria, 1984.

Chong, S.P, *The Music of the Soul: A pathway to a rich and fulfilling life*, Sidharta Publishers, Melbourne, Australia, 2011.

Chong, S.P, *The Book of Testaments: A practical guide for spiritual realization*, Boolarong Press, Brisbane, Australia, 2009.

Cole, K, *Management: Theory and Practice*, Pearson Education Australia, 2005.

Cole, K, *Supervision: The theory and practice of first-line management*, Pearson Education Australia, 2001.

Encarta English Dictionary, on-line edition 2011.

Frankl, V.E, *Man's Search For Meaning*, Random House Group, 1959.

Griffiths, B, *Return to the Centre*, Harper Collins Publishers, London, 1978.

Herman, J.L, *Trauma and Recovery: From Domestic Abuse to Political Terror*, Rivers Oram Press, London, 1992.

http://www.brainyquote.com/quotes/authors/j/joseph_campbell.html, accessed 5 November 2012

http://plato.stanford.edu/entries/freewill/, accessed 10 May 2011

http://www.businessdictionary.com/definition/values.html, accessed 5 April 2011

http://teenagebrain.blogspot.com/ The Teenage Brain, accessed 6 May 2011

Jeffares, A.N. & Gray M, *Dictionary of Quotations*, Harper Collins Publishers, Glasgow, 1995.

Kubler-Ross, E. (1997) *The Wheel of Life: A Memoir of Living and*

Dying, Bantam Press, 1997.

Kuik, A, *The Search for Oneness*, Connect magazine, edition 78, Cairns, Australia, March 2011.

Poland, T. D, *WHK Accelerator Program, Entrepreneurs Success Program*, Australia, 2008.

Oxford English Reference Dictionary, 1995.

Rinpoche, S, *The Tibetan Book of Living and Dying*, Harper Collins Publishers Inc, 1992.

Ricard, M, *Happiness: A Guide to Developing Life's most important skill*, Atlantic Books, London, 2003.

Sanchez, N. & Vieira, T, *Take Me To Truth*, O Books, Ropley, UK, 2007.

Seligman, M.E.P, *Authentic Happiness*, Random Press, 2002.

Shaw, C, *How To Get More Nookie*, FC Productions, Australia, 2012.

The Stanford Encyclopaedia of Philosophy, (accessed 10.5.11).

Truman, K.K, *Feelings: Buried alive never die*, Olympus Distributing, Las Vegas, Nevada, 1991.

Walsch, N.D, *Home with God: A Life That Never Ends*, Atria Books, 2006.

Walsch, N.D, *Friendship with God: An uncommon dialogue*, Hodder and Stoughton, 1999.

Walsch, N.D, *Conversations with God: An uncommon dialogue, Book 3*, Hampton Roads Publishing Company, 1998.

Walsch, N.D, *The New Revelations: A Conversation with God*, Atria Books, 2002.

Walsch, N.D, *Conversations with God: An uncommon dialogue – living in the world with honesty, courage and love*, Hampton Roads Publishing Company, VA. 1997.

Wheeler, C.M. MD, PH.D, *Ten simple solutions to stress*, pp. 124, New Harbinger Publications, Oakland, CA, 2007.

Wikipedia (http://en.wikipedia.org/wiki/Truth, accessed April 2011).

BOOKS

O is a symbol of the world, of oneness and unity. In different cultures it also means the "eye," symbolizing knowledge and insight. We aim to publish books that are accessible, constructive and that challenge accepted opinion, both that of academia and the "moral majority."

Our books are available in all good English language bookstores worldwide. If you don't see the book on the shelves ask the bookstore to order it for you, quoting the ISBN number and title. Alternatively you can order online (all major online retail sites carry our titles) or contact the distributor in the relevant country, listed on the copyright page.

See our website **www.o-books.net** for a full list of over 500 titles, growing by 100 a year.

And tune in to myspiritradio.com for our book review radio show, hosted by June-Elleni Laine, where you can listen to the authors discussing their books.

MySpiritRadio